T0418633

Towards a Harmonic Grammar of Grieg's Late Piano Music

The music of Edvard Grieg is justly celebrated for its harmonic richness, a feature especially apparent in the piano works written in the last decades of his life. Grieg was enchanted by what he styled the 'dreamworld' of harmony, a magical realm whose principles the composer felt remained a mystery even to himself, and he was not alone, in that the complex nature of late-Romantic harmony around 1900 has proved a keen source of debate up to the present day. Grieg's music forms a particularly profitable repertoire for focusing current debates about the nature of tonality and tonal harmony. Departing from earlier approaches, this study is not simply an inventory of Griegian harmonic traits but seeks rather to ascertain the deeper principles at work governing their meaningful conjunction, how elements of Grieg's harmonic grammar are utilised in creating an extended tonal syntax. Building both on historical theories and more recent developments, Benedict Taylor develops new models for understanding the complexity of late-Romantic tonal practice as epitomised in Grieg's music. Such an investigation casts further valuable light on the twin issues of nature and nationalism long connected with the composer: the question of tonality as something natural or culturally constructed and larger historiographical claims concerning Grieg's apparent position on the periphery of the Austro-German tradition.

Benedict Taylor is Chancellor's Fellow in the Reid School of Music, University of Edinburgh. He is the author of *Mendelssohn, Time and Memory: The Romantic Conception of Cyclic Form* (Cambridge, 2011) and *The Melody of Time: Music and Temporality in the Romantic Era,* (Oxford, 2016).

ROYAL MUSICAL ASSOCIATION MONOGRAPHS

General Editor: Simon P. Keefe

This series is supported by funds made available to the Royal Musical Association from the estate of Thurston Dart, former King Edward Professor of Music at the University of London. The editorial board is the Publications Committee of the Association.

Recent monographs in the series (for a full list, see the end of this book):

Skryabin, Philosophy and the Music of Desire (2012)
Kenneth M. Smith

The politics of plainchant in fin-de-siècle France (2013)
Katharine Ellis

Brahms Beyond Mastery: His Sarabande and Gavotte, and its Recompositions (2013)
Robert Pascall

Regina Mingotti: Diva and Impresario at the King's Theatre, London (2013)
Michael Burden

Heinrich Schenker and Beethoven's 'Hammerklavier' Sonata (2013)
Nicholas Marston

The Politics of Verdi's Cantica (2014)
Roberta Montemorra Marvin

Johann Mattheson's Pièces de clavecin and Das neu-eröffnete Orchestre (2014)
Margaret Seares

Singing Dante: The Literary Origins of Cinquecento Monody (2014)
Elena Abramov-van Rijk

The 'Ars musica' Attributed to Magister Lambertus/Aristoteles (2015)
Christian Meyer, editor and Karen Desmond, translator

Magister Jacobus de Ispania, author of the Speculum musicae (2015)
Margaret Bent

Towards a Harmonic Grammar of Grieg's Late Piano Music (2016)
Benedict Taylor

The Genesis and Development of an English Organ Sonata (2016)
Iain Quinn

Towards a Harmonic Grammar of Grieg's Late Piano Music

Nature and Nationalism

BENEDICT TAYLOR

LONDON AND NEW YORK

First published 2017
by Routledge
2 Park Square, Milton Park, Abingdon, Oxon OX14 4RN

and by Routledge
711 Third Avenue, New York, NY 10017

Routledge is an imprint of the Taylor & Francis Group, an informa business

British Library Cataloguing-in-Publication Data
A catalogue record for this book is available from the British Library

Library of Congress Cataloging-in-Publication Data
Names: Taylor, Benedict, 1981-
Title: Towards a harmonic grammar of Grieg's late piano music: nature and nationalism / Benedict Taylor.
Description: Abingdon, Oxon; New York, NY: Routledge, 2016. | Includes bibliographical references and index.
Identifiers: LCCN 2016035300| ISBN 9781472456588 (hardback: alk. paper) | ISBN 9781315307350 (ebook)
Subjects: LCSH: Grieg, Edvard, 1843-1907. Piano music. | Grieg, Edvard, 1843-1907—Harmony. | Piano music—19th century—Analysis, apperciation.
Classification: LCC ML410.G9 T39 2016 | DDC 786.2092—dc23
LC record available at https://lccn.loc.gov/2016035300

ISBN: 978-1-472-45658-8 (hbk)
ISBN: 978-1-315-30735-0 (ebk)

Typeset in Palatino Linotype
by codeMantra

Printed in the United Kingdom
by Henry Ling Limited

* * *

Contents

List of figures

List of music examples

Acknowledgements

It was the work of Edvard Grieg that first drew me towards music many years ago, and thus writing this book was in many ways a return to a first love, one that had not dimmed in the interim. I may have grown out of the tendency to compose music consisting almost solely of interminably slipping chromatic harmonies, but my desire to understand why Grieg's worked, whereas mine never did, was a guiding stimulus behind this study. Like Grieg, I am still baffled by the dreamworld of harmony, but I hope that a few pointers have been set out here within this mysterious terrain, ones which may elucidate aspects of Grieg's music just as they might – being hopelessly optimistic – suggest further possible courses for compositional endeavours.

Although it had long been on my mind to write a study of Grieg, this project was finally made possible by a Mellon Postdoctoral Fellowship at the University of Oxford in 2012–13 and written during the unusually wintery month of March 2013, and I would especially like to thank Daniel Grimley, Jonathan Cross and Eric Clarke for supporting this fellowship. In particular, Dan has been a constant inspiration through his pioneering work on Grieg and Scandinavian music and an ever-helpful colleague whose knowledge of this repertoire is seemingly endless. The present account has benefited immeasurably from his input. Several years before at Princeton, Dmitri Tymoczko had stimulated several of the theoretical lines of inquiry found here, besides being admirably curious to explore this often-overlooked repertoire, and gave kind feedback on the draft of this book. Going even further back, Dean Sutcliffe, my undergraduate director of studies, first revealed how much there was to say about Grieg's music with his now legendary analysis supervision on 'Klokkeklang' (I now in turn have inflicted this piece on a future generation of undergraduates, though without the same skill or exacting precision as Dean). To my brother Nathaniel and his family I owe thanks for helping make some sense of some of the more obscure Norwegian dialects I encountered along the way, and perhaps even more importantly, shared memories of a distant trip to Norway in which the Hardangerfjord, Bergen and Troldhaugen were encountered in a miraculous June sunshine. (Such clemency, I have since learned, should not be expected in that part of the world.) To my brother Damian I owe gratitude again for his careful and patient reading that has saved this book from a number of errors.

Musical examples contained within this study are primarily based on scores published in the *Grieg Gesamtausgabe* (*GGA*): Edvard Grieg, *Samlede Verker* (Frankfurt: C.F. Peters, 1977–95). However, in a number of instances errors have been inadvertently introduced into this critical edition that were not present in earlier editions, and thus such mistakes have been tacitly rectified wherever identified. The transcription of these examples has been expertly done by Jake Spence, and made possible by a subvention from the American Musicological Society's Joseph Kerman Endowment. I would also like to express my deep gratitude to Siren Steen and the Bergen Public Library for their kind permission to reproduce extracts from Frants Beyer's original transcription of the melodies used by Grieg in his Op. 66 collection. Finally, Simon Keefe has been an ideally helpful and generous series editor for RMA Monographs and I would like to express my sincere thanks for the support he has shown for this volume.

Introduction

Enticements

The opening 'Kulokk' from Grieg's *19 Norske Folkeviser*, Op. 66, forms a fittingly sonorous starting point for this late piano collection of 1896–7. A miniature of particular yet unassuming beauty, the apparent simplicity of this piece is deceptive. Within its brief twenty bars this example contains many of the distinctive elements that make up Grieg's mature harmonic style (Ex. 0.1a).

Example 0.1a Edvard Grieg, 'Kulokk', *19 Norwegian Folksongs*, Op. 66 No. 1

The opening chord resonates with a wonderfully warm sonority; analytical description barely conveys how the harmony simply glows when played on the piano. Grieg's spacing of the D major chord clearly reflects the natural overtones of the harmonic series, but there is something about the tessitura chosen that imparts the particular inner radiance to the sound produced. Above this harmonic foundation the treble's opening melodic figure – the actual *kulokk* ('cow-call', more literally 'cow enticement') promised in the work's title – enters, suspended from the sixth scale degree b^2, the highest pitch in the piece heard simultaneously against the lowest. Resolving as an appoggiatura to $\hat{5}$ and continuing as if free of measure down notes drawn from the D major arpeggio, the implicit pentatonic colouring of this motive suggests a folk-like or 'natural' tincture (*Siegfried*'s woodbird might be called to mind). The initial added sixth sounding above the bass, aided by the sustained reverberation created by the pedalling, forms a gently impressionistic sonority that seems to fold in on itself, one that, like the naturalistic call of the title, entices us into the dreamworld of Griegian harmony.[1] The allure of such a realm is subtly enacted by the yearning quality physically conveyed in performance by the two-octave leap in the right hand from the opening low f♯ to this b^2 above. No less significantly, the gap created between the bass's D and the b^2 in the treble three and a half octaves higher opens up a registral space that the subsequent course of the piece will ingeniously and systematically fill.

The fourteen bars that form the central section of the piece harmonise a simple folk-tune that, as Dag Schjelderup-Ebbe has observed, with the exception of the embellishing upper neighbour-note G and a solitary passing C♯ is entirely restricted to a pentatonic collection.[2] In fact the melody is little more than a succession of ornamented repetitions of a three-note ascending figure d^2–e^2–f♯^{2}, subjected to an unselfconscious principle of developing-variation. For instance the anacrusic sixth beat, filled in at b. 4 with an ornamented passing note e^2 that balances the ascending three-note figure with its mirror inversion, gives rise to a stronger syncopated emphasis on this pitch in b. 5; the ornamental triplet formula is then extended in the consequent phrase formed by bb. 7–11 before being reconfigured as the extended upbeat to the climactic phrase at b. 12. Such is the continual variation so created that it is not until six bars into this highly repetitive design that a melodic unit is reheard in exactly corresponding form (b. 8 mirroring b. 4). Nonetheless, there is still a clear sense of higher-level repetition within the phrase, working architectonically beneath the evolving linear process. Beyond the initial sense

[1] The term 'dreamworld' (*Traumwelt*) is Grieg's own, used with specific reference to his Op. 66 collection (as discussed below).

[2] Dag Schjelderup-Ebbe, *A Study of Grieg's Harmony, with Special Reference to His Contributions to Musical Impressionism* (Oslo: J.G. Tanum, 1953), p. 42.

of periodicity created between bb. 3–6 and 7–11, the tail-figure of bb. 10–11 – an appended b^1–a^1 suspension harking back to the opening cow-calling figure – breaks the entire *kulokk* into two larger, unequal parts, with the second (bb. 12–16) formed from the abridged and modified repetition of the end of the first. It is all the more notable, then, that despite the apparently artful, almost Brahmsian quality of this design, Grieg is simply remaining true to the original melody, as notated by his friend Frants Beyer following a walking tour the two shared in the Jotunheimen mountain region in Western Norway (Ex. 0.1b).

Example 0.1b *Kulokk* melody of Grieg's Op. 66 No. 1, in the original transcription by Frants Beyer. (Grieg Archive, Bergen Public Library, mb op. 66 [Tekst og skisser til folkeviser som inngår i op. 66])

The most evident feature in Grieg's harmonisation of this melody is its construction around a large-scale descending diatonic line in the bass, normally paralleled in tenths with an inner voice. This feature is manifest in the scalic descent from the d^1 in b. 7 to the F♯ in b. 13, to which the E of bb. 14–15 and final D of b. 17 clearly belong, albeit now separated by the interspersed notes from the prominent cycle of fifths presented in root position, which now takes over as the constructive principle. Thus the bass's initial two-octave leap in bb. 1–3 is smoothly filled in through every intervening diatonic note across the ensuing seventeen bars.[3] This descent is already nascent, though, in the parallel inner-voice movement in the melody's first four bars, from which it emerges as a registrally expanding outgrowth.

For the initial $\hat{1}$ in the melody the downbeat of b. 3 is harmonised by Grieg with a IV^6_4 in place of the more readily expected tonic. A moment of colour that softens the music with a subdominant tinge, the prominent $\hat{6}$ in this chord could also be a reflection of the first melodic event of the piece, the b^3 of b. 1. However, rather than resolving down as a simple plagal-like $^6_4$–$^5_3$ suspension (as the behaviour of the opening appoggiatura would suggest), the thirds in the inner voices shift *up* a

[3] The entire registral space of the piece is in fact filled out, as the b^2 and a^2 of the opening *kulokk* connect to the g^2 mordent to the f♯^{2} in b. 3, from which pitch one may trace a number of larger descending lines running through Grieg's texture.

diatonic step to $^{7}_{5}$, followed by another step to $^{8}_{6}$, before the process circles around on itself. Evidently the mildly recalcitrant inner voices decline to resolve to a state of harmonic ease; the plagal cadence implicit in b. 3, and the harmonic release onto the tonic that would come with it, is not realised.

As if resulting from the accumulated harmonic and linear tension of these opening bars, the one hitherto stable element, the bass's tonic pedal, now moves. It effectively splits into two voices: the tenor remains steadily holding the d^1 pedal while the bass takes over the conjunct movement formerly confined to the inner voices. Alternatively, read in more linear fashion, a voice-exchange may be posited in b. 7 between the tenor's otherwise unresolving g^1 and the treble's ensuing $f\sharp^2$, the melody's d^2 at the start of the bar being taken down an octave into the bass voice. Either way, the result is the momentary replacement of the conjunct parallel thirds with sixths for a bar, before tenths reassert themselves at b. 8^4. From this point to the attainment of a structurally decisive tonic $^{6}_{3}$ at b. 13, the lower voices move in a recurring 4–5 linear intervallic pattern across the span of an octave and a half. What first appeared as a colouristic local oscillation in the inner voices comes to take over the texture and registral space of the piece, emerging as the decisive motivating factor in the work's formal process.

The final, climactic stage of the setting is reached in b. 13 as systematised linear succession gives way to strong cadential movement through the cycle of fifths. The progressive descent has gained increasing momentum and harmonic tension, forces that are concentrated in the diatonic half-diminished vii^{4}_{3} of b. 12^4, which well-nigh inevitably falls to the tonic first inversion, coinciding with the reintroduction of the melody's second half. An $a\sharp$ in the alto line significantly marks the first manifestation of chromaticism, forming an augmented triad on I easily reinterpreted through its constituent intervallic equivalency as a chromatically altered V^{6-5}/VI based on root III, thus leading smoothly to the VI of b. 14 and with it the cycle of fifths VI–II^9–[$^{6}_{4}$]–V^9–[I]. By eliding the resolution of the dominant-functioning VI with a further secondary seventh on II Grieg springs two steps forward in one movement, yet by leaving the $f\sharp^2$ of b. 14 hanging across to the next E^7 harmony he creates a sensuous major ninth from the tardy resolution of the previous chord.[4] A new common-time variant of the tail-figure from bb. 10–11 is fused with the $[V]^{6}_{4}$–V^9 harmony that seems to lead us, finally, to the tonic that has for so long been withheld. This is the point where the melody, in Beyer's transcription, breaks off, left dangling on $\hat{6}$.

Harmonically and melodically, we feel the music's need to resolve the b^1 $\hat{6}$ down to the a^1 $\hat{5}$, corresponding to the earlier appearance of this melodic paradigm in bb. 10–11, alongside a perfect cadential

[4] The melodic line is extended by a full bar here, the $f\sharp^2$ occupying eleven beats in Grieg's version to the five given in Beyer's transcription.

progression resolving the V^9 chord to I. We might also recall the reiterated IV^6_4 harmonies in the opening passage that had all along held out the promise of plagal resolution, one that has so far been denied. Grieg grants us a perfect cadence of sorts, and this long-sought $\hat{6}$–$\hat{5}$ resolution too, but in both cases this is accomplished through unexpected means. For this melodic and harmonic cadential longing is met with the return of the cow-calling motive of the opening bars – an addition of Grieg's to the notated folk-tune that interposes the melody as such within this wider frame. The composer steps forward as it were to complete what nature (or at any rate the herding girl) had left open and incomplete.

The high b^2–a^2 of the *kulokk* motive both resolves the melodic line an octave above and reengages the registral space left at the opening, just as the bass's D completes the large-scale linear descent by similarly reattaining the pitch formed by its starting point. Its opening motivically redefined through this adroit linkage technique, the final pitch of this *kulokk* figure now finds an unexpected functional use. As we have glimpsed, register and line appear to be of great importance in Grieg's music, and here the a^1 crucially completes the $\hat{6}$–$\hat{5}$ motion left open by the b^1 of b. 16, back in the correct register. Harmonically, meanwhile, the cycle of fifths overshoots the tonic by turning it into a ninth chord – the dominant of its subdominant. (The impressionistic clime of the resulting six-note sonority, with the added sixth high above, is even more pronounced than in the beginning.) And yet this subdominant leaning – a tendency which, as Kurt von Fischer has shown, runs throughout the piece at the expense of dominant and tonic affirmation alike – acts now as the means for resolving this aspect of the piece's harmonic organisation.[5] For in these last two bars the plagal implication the melody's initial harmonisation and melodic concentration on $\hat{6}$ had lead us to expect is finally realised, balancing the registral separation of the *kulokk* gesture and its underpinning harmony by being stated in the keyboard's warm middle range. The formal rounding off provided by the return of the opening bars simultaneously elides with the cadential course of the intervening melody and resourcefully completes its process. There is a sense of resolution and peace to these bars, the fulfilment of what was always promised but until now withheld.

From the analysis above one may identify three distinct elements that constitute Grieg's harmonic resource in this piece: the emphasis on *Klang*, on the sensuous quality of sound in itself, as evidenced in the added-sixth sonority and resonant spacing of the opening and closing bars; the strongly profiled, systematic linear writing of the scalic descent that takes up the greater part of the piece; and finally the functional fifth progression brought into use on nearing the final cadence. Yet as was shown, this functionality, already decorated by the colouristic use of secondary and dominant ninths, is simultaneously overrun

[5] Kurt von Fischer, *Griegs Harmonik und die nordländische Folklore* (Bern and Leipzig: Paul Haupt, 1938), pp. 14–15, 18.

and undercut by the elided cadence onto the tonic ninth in b. 17, the recall of the opening sonority, and a final, dominant-denying plagal cadence. With this return, too, harmonic and linear/registral processes, set up in the opening bars, find their final resolution. The three elements defined above become interlaced as part of a broader process that mixes traditional tonal progression with colouristic and systematic elements of more Romantic, impressionist, or even proto-modernist provenance. We move from an examination of individual principles of harmonic construction to an account of their functional interrelation: an exploration of Griegian harmonic grammar becomes comingled with an account of Griegian syntax.

Grieg and Late-Romantic Harmony: Theoretical and Historiographical Concerns

The example of Op. 66 No. 1 just given serves as a useful prism for isolating key aspects of Grieg's harmonic language and showing how these diverse grammatical elements interact in a syntactically meaningful manner – the concerns, in short, of the present study. Indeed, the collection from which this 'Kulokk' is drawn, the *19 Norwegian Folksongs*, Op. 66, forms an apt starting point for a larger consideration of harmony in Grieg's music. This set in fact inspired one of Grieg's best-known statements on the nature of his involvement with the world of harmony:

> The realm of harmonies has always been my dreamworld, and the relation between my harmonic way of feeling and Norwegian folk-tunes was a mystery even to myself. I have found that the obscure depth of our melodies has its foundation in their wealth of undreamt-of harmonic possibilities. In my Op. 66 arrangements of folksongs and elsewhere, I have sought to give an expression to my awareness of the hidden harmonies of our folk-tunes. To this end in particular the chromatic lines in the harmonic texture have strongly attracted me.[6]

Notably, however, Grieg is not only speaking of his fascination with harmony but moreover confessing his bafflement at how to explain this feature more theoretically. Despite being christened in the year that Op. 66 was conceived as one of the two 'greatest creators of harmony of the present day', Grieg himself prefaces the oft-used quotation with

[6] Grieg, letter to Henry Theophilus Finck, 17 July 1900 ('das Reich der Harmonien war immer meine Traumwelt und das Verhältnis meiner harmonischen Empfindungsweise zu der norwegischen Volksweise war mir selbst ein Mysterium. Ich habe gefunden, das[s] die dunkle Tiefe unserer Weisen in deren Reichtum an ungeahnten harmonischen Möglichkeiten ihren Grund hat. In meiner Bearbeitung der Volkslieder Op. 68 [recte 66] und auch sonst, habe ich es versucht, meine Ahnung von den verborgenen Harmonien unseres Volkstones einen Ausdruck zu geben. Für diesen Zweck haben mich ganz besonders die chromatischen Tonfolgen im harmonischen Gewebe stark angezogen'), German original in *Artikler og taler*, ed. Øystein Gaukstad (Oslo: Gyldendal, 1957), pp. 51–2. An alternative translation can be found in *Edvard Grieg: Letters to Colleagues and Friends*, ed. and trans. Finn Benestad and William H. Halverson (Columbus, OH: Peer Gynt Press, 2000), p. 229.

the assertion 'to talk about harmonic innovations is difficult for me'.[7] Harmony was evidently something which puzzled him just as much as it does musicians and scholars to this day.

For contemporary theorists still frequently profess their fascination and bewilderment with the harmonic language of late-nineteenth-century music.[8] Beyond the evident richness and complexity of late-Romantic harmonic practice, the question over to what extent examples from this period exhibit tonal properties, indeed what exactly constitutes tonality, stands not always helpfully as a conceptual limiting factor behind any discussion. There is a nagging suspicion that 'tonality', inevitably defined in opposition to 'atonality' (rather than modality) since the latter term was coined, often serves as little more than a narrow ideological category, one which pays scant regard to the sheer plurality of elements that make up what common usage designates as 'tonal music'. Often a multitude of different, contrasting techniques seem to be implicated by this repertoire. The positing of a 'second practice' has helped establish a basis for many harmonic traits that, while departing from classical practice, are common in later nineteenth-century usage,[9] and recently great developments have been made in related theories that may broadly be termed 'Neo-Riemannian', created to deal with highly chromatic though nonetheless triadically based music.[10] But as Grieg's music readily demonstrates, music which is unquestionably tonal in much of its rhetoric and functional behaviour may display harmonic attributes that cannot be reduced to either a functional first practice or the triadic chromaticism of a second, alternative tradition – nor, even, to their juxtaposition and constant

[7] 'über harmonische Neuerungen zu reden, fällt mir schwer', *Artikler og taler*, p. 51; the earlier writer was Frank J. Sawyer, in 'The Tendencies of Modern Harmony as Exemplified in the Works of Dvořák and Grieg', *Proceedings of the Musical Association*, 22 (1895–6), 86.

[8] See for instance Daniel Harrison, *Harmonic Function in Chromatic Music: A Renewed Dualist Theory and an Account of Its Precedents* (Chicago: University of Chicago Press, 1994), p. ix; Anthony Pople, 'Using Complex Set Theory for Tonal Analysis: An Introduction to the *Tonalities* Project', *Music Analysis*, 23 (2004), 153; Dmitri Tymoczko, *A Geometry of Music: Harmony and Counterpoint in the Extended Common Practice* (New York: Oxford University Press, 2011), p. xviii.

[9] The notion of a second practice of 'chromatic tonality' in the nineteenth century (contrasting with earlier 'diatonic tonality') was formulated by Gregory Proctor in 'Technical Bases of Nineteenth-Century Chromatic Tonality' (PhD diss., Princeton University, 1978), pp. 130–250, and the term 'second practice' brought into common analytic currency in the work of scholars following the lines of inquiry set out by Robert Bailey; see especially the essays collected in William Kinderman and Harald Krebs (eds.), *The Second Practice of Nineteenth-Century Tonality* (Lincoln: University of Nebraska Press, 1996).

[10] See especially the pioneering work of David Lewin, Brian Hyer, Daniel Harrison, Richard Cohn, and more recent developments from scholars such as David Kopp, Julian Hook and Steven Rings. The contemporary breadth of this field is demonstrated by Edward Gollin and Alexander Rehding (eds.), *The Oxford Handbook of Neo-Riemannian Music Theories* (New York: Oxford University Press, 2011).

mediation.[11] An inventory of Griegian harmonic elements, reduced to the fewest distinct genera, could well include the following traits:

- First-practice functional harmony: cycles of fifths, functional root progressions.
- Second-practice triadic chromaticism: chromatic or parsimonious voice leading, mediant shifts and common-tone modulation.
- Modality and other types of scalar modulation. Broadly understood, this category could expand to include the use of the minor dominant (especially in the major), plagal cadences, and falling leading-note motion ($\hat{7}$–$\hat{6}$–$\hat{5}$), which soften dominant functionality.
- Extended tonal harmony: supra-triadic entities, added-note chords, pandiatonicism, alongside a related delight in *Klang* as a constitutive element in its own right.
- Systematisation, especially of lines (whether chromatic, scalar, or through some other interval cycle), often allied to a marked sensitivity to register. The use of pedals may also be included here. This category may furthermore be applied to those above, resulting in such features as the systematic exploration of fifth cycles, chromatic lines, or the construction of higher-order tertiary entities.

One might of course argue that after the first two categories only the fourth strictly constitutes a tonal property, as modality and related types of scalar procedure are pre-tonal, and the systematisation of pitch progression suggests a modernist, quasi-atonal procedure often based around the measure of the chromatic scale-step as fundamental unit. (From a hard-line perspective, say that of Heinrich Schenker, even the second and fourth types would be debatable inclusions.) But for the latter-day theorist or historian interested in accounting for what attributes have been commonly accepted as constituting tonality, rather than delimiting the concept to support a particularly narrow, essentialist agenda of aesthetic inclusion and exclusion, the properties above may surely relate to tonal behaviour as generally understood, and certainly as manifested in Grieg's oeuvre.

What is needed, I would suggest, is a more flexible and inclusive conception of what this elusive idea of tonality might entail. One possible basis for such an approach is that provided by the recent work on the geometrical foundations of Western harmony by Dmitri Tymoczko, who proposes that tonality, understood broadly, may consist of five general features or components.[12] These are, respectively:

- conjunct melodic motion
- acoustic consonance

[11] See for instance Richard Cohn's recent contention that late-Romantic harmonic practice formed a bilingual system capable of switching effortlessly between first and second practices (*Audacious Euphony: Chromatic Harmony and the Triad's Second Nature* (New York: Oxford University Press, 2012), pp. 199–210).

[12] Tymoczko, *A Geometry of Music*, pp. 3–27, esp. 4–7.

- harmonic consistency
- limited macroharmony
- centricity.

Tymoczko contends that these features may be present, to greater or lesser degrees and manifested in different forms, in an extended tradition of tonal common practice stretching in the West from medieval times to present-day pop and jazz, and moreover in much non-Western music. As will be seen, Tymoczko's perspective on the harmonic qualities associated with tonality, broadly defined, may offer an extremely useful starting point for understanding certain aspects of Grieg's practice.

Returning to historical concerns, part of the problem in accounting for tonality and its associated harmonic practices is, as implied before, historiographical and ideological. Both of the governing narratives familiar to the twentieth century concerning tonality – one simply telling of its rise in the eighteenth century followed by its deplorable decline by the end of the nineteenth (a theme notably rehearsed by Schenker), the other reinterpreting this scheme as one of historically inevitable evolution through the increased chromaticism of the nineteenth century's second practice to atonality (an idea of distinct Schoenbergian provenance) – make no space for broader alternatives to understanding tonality and the range of harmonic practices around 1900. Closely bound up with such readings are two important notions that will feature, either implicitly or explicitly, throughout much of this following study: the question of nationality (which may quickly turn into one of nationalism), and the appeal to nature as a foundation for tonality.

The first idea, nationality or nationalism, underpins the problematic notion of a musical 'mainstream' and its geographical locus in the music of Austro-German composers, a grand narrative common in the nineteenth and early twentieth centuries but one whose historical determinism and ethnocentric bias have appeared increasingly dubious to late-twentieth-century tastes. In an illuminating chapter on the historically unstable concept of 'tonality', Brian Hyer pertinently comments that

> The notion of an evolution in tonal music tends to compress the messy diversity of contemporaneous compositional practices into a single historical mainstream.... As a result, accounts of musical evolution smooth over historical discontinuities, either failing to register divergent practices or dismissing them as inconsequential departures from the main music-historical current.[13]

In our post-modern outlook (which admittedly is no less determined by historical and cultural factors) we are now more likely to insist on

[13] Brian Hyer, 'Tonality', in Thomas Christensen (ed.), *The Cambridge History of Western Music Theory* (Cambridge: Cambridge University Press, 2002), p. 746.

the irreducible plurality of practices and geographically diverse *petites histoires*. But in Grieg's day and for much of intervening century it was the Austro-German tradition that coursed most strongly through the historiography of music, and thus any music originating outside this geographic centre (which would hence be termed 'nationalist', in opposition to a supposedly universal German idiom) and which did not fit with its dominant narratives concerning the development of tonality could well be ignored.

A related point, on which the implicitly Germanocentric argument for musical supremacy often bases its justification, is the idea of 'nature': whether tonality possesses an intrinsically natural foundation or not. The connexion between musical harmony and the natural overtone series has been known since the time of Pythagoras and underpinned Rameau's theory of the *basse fondamentale*, but certainly from Moritz Hauptmann onward the appeal to nature becomes a primary argument and ultimate authority for tonality in German music theory.[14] Theorists in the later nineteenth and early twentieth centuries disputed to what extent tonality was a natural system – the highest, most nearly perfect historical development of music – rather than a product of human artifice and ingenuity which at best, under certain conditions, approximated a natural basis in the overtone series and differed from one age and land to another. Figures like Arthur von Oettingen and Heinrich Schenker were aligned more to the first, absolutist camp, Hermann von Helmholtz and Arnold Schoenberg to the implicit historical and cultural relativism of the second (though the latter was nonetheless not immune from appealing to the determination of historical necessity when it suited him). Many theorists, meanwhile – Hauptmann and Hugo Riemann to name two more prominent examples – occupied an uncomfortable and shifting no-mans-land between the two outposts of nature and culture. Any aspect of tonality (such as the major triad) that could be grounded in an appeal to natural properties was readily adduced as evidence of its innately natural quality and laws, but other more obdurate facets (such as the minor mode) created greater problems for naturalistic explanation. To the modern outlook, predictably, it is the absolutist-leaning perspective that appears the more untenable. Hyer, again, argues that 'the history of tonality is better understood in terms of specific harmonic practices rather than immutable laws', and the more cautious and historically nuanced empiricism of the second, relativist position certainly seems the more prudent – if less ambitious – course to adopt.[15]

[14] On the varied historical byways between music theory and nature see especially the essays collected in Suzannah Clark and Alexander Rehding (eds.), *Music Theory and Natural Order from the Renaissance to the Early Twentieth Century* (Cambridge: Cambridge University Press, 2001).

[15] Hyer, 'Tonality', p. 746.

Harmony, Nationalism and Nature: The Case of Grieg

The music of Edvard Grieg (1843–1907) would appear to be a particularly promising example to use as a case-study to explore the 'messy diversity' of late-nineteenth-century harmonic practices, offering an alternative music-historical narrative to the familiar Germanocentric chromatic tradition of Wagner and Schoenberg. Grieg provides an ideal instance of a contemporaneous composer noted for his harmonic legerdemain whose music is historically bound up with the issues of nature and nationalism: the questions of culture versus nature and centre versus periphery. That Grieg's compositional output is closely linked with his status as a nationalist composer, someone dwelling on the fringes of the Austro-German musical empire, in no way forms a peripheral part of his appeal but in fact constitutes almost the essence of his reputation. The familiar nationalistic narrative was even constructed by the composer's own accounts of his development, whereby four years in the traditional heartland of German musical culture, Leipzig, is supposed to have equipped him with next to nothing worthwhile, before an encounter with the young Norwegian firebrand Rikard Nordraak in Copenhagen set him on the true path to musical identity – national self-determination through an alliance with Norwegian folk music. Grieg thus self-consciously articulates his peripheral status vis-à-vis a German mainstream; indeed a large part of his public appeal has been through the picturesque associations with an apparently peculiarly Norwegian variety of musical exoticism.[16] Although such an alliance has arguably paid rich dividends among the music-loving public, it is noticeable that while Grieg may have received some attention from scholars in his time, his neglect among more recent music theorists might in fact stem from this very aspect.[17]

Furthermore, within this nationalistic context the distinction between nature and its other, culture, plays an especially significant part in Grieg's aesthetics and reception. The putative Norwegian quality of Grieg's music is inextricably entwined with notions of nature and – that apparently only mildly more artificial category of the nineteenth-century mind – the native folk with their natural, guileless melodies. 'Fresh from the cow' joked Grieg's friend Frants Beyer when transcribing in the field the melodies contained in Op. 66, propping

[16] One of the first mildly sceptical and revisionist accounts of the Norwegian nationalist narrative was provided by Dag Schjelderup-Ebbe in *Edvard Grieg, 1858–1867: With Special Reference to the Evolution of His Harmonic Style* (Oslo/London: Universitetsforlaget/Allen & Unwin, 1964). Daniel M. Grimley explores the issues of Norwegian identity, nationalism and exoticism in significantly greater depth in *Grieg: Music, Landscape and Norwegian Identity* (Woodbridge: Boydell and Brewer, 2006).

[17] Two prominent examples from the early twentieth century of theorists treating Grieg's harmonic innovations with a degree of respect are Georg Capellen and Ernst Kurth. Yet one looks in vain for extended treatment of Grieg's harmony in most theorists stemming from the Schenkerian, Schoenbergian, Fortean or even Neo-Riemannian traditions in post-war Anglo-American music theory.

his manuscript paper against a bovine backrest in order to capture the singing of Jotunheimen herd-girls in all its artless immediacy.[18]

In fact this purported connexion between harmonic development and nature is present particularly strongly in the composer's Op. 66. Commentators have long agreed that this set is especially rich harmonically, even by Grieg's standards. In his early inventory of Griegian harmonic practice Dag Schjelderup-Ebbe describes the collection as 'one of the high points of Grieg's harmonic writing, [in which] all resources of late-nineteenth-century harmony are taken into use'.[19] In the later, standard biography of the composer Schjelderup-Ebbe wrote in conjunction with Finn Benestad, this evaluation is elaborated upon:

> What strikes one most of all about these arrangements is the exceptionally rich harmony...The spectrum of harmonic means is broader than in Grieg's earlier works...The advanced harmonic means he had developed – such as parallel chords, long series of altered chords, unusual cadences, and veiled tonality – were worked into these arrangements in the most natural manner.[20]

The closing line – 'most natural manner' – is probably not intended to call up the idea of nature in the more literal sense, but nonetheless does link to the use of this category in the composer's own accounts of his creative encounter with Norwegian folk music as documented by Op. 66. For in his own statements on this collection Grieg concurs with later audiences in their impression of harmonic daring, but significantly adds a naturalistic, even mildly mystical cause for this quality. In a letter to his friend Julius Röntgen, written during the summer of 1896 as he was at work on the set, Grieg claims

> I have indeed put some hair-raising harmonic combinations to paper. But by way of excuse let it be said that they weren't created at the piano but in my head. When one has the Vøring Falls close by one feels more independent and daring than down in the valley.[21]

[18] The witticism ('Frisch von der Kuh') is related by Julius Röntgen, *Grieg* (The Hague: J. Philip Kruseman, 1930), p. 33 (though in an interview in the *Nieuwe Rotterdamsche Courant*, 7 May 1930, Röntgen attributes it to Grieg himself).

[19] Dag Schjelderup-Ebbe, *A Study of Grieg's Harmony*, p. 160.

[20] Finn Benestad and Dag Schjelderup-Ebbe, *Edvard Grieg: The Man and the Artist*, trans. William H. Halverson and Leland B. Sateren (Gloucester: Alan Sutton, 1988), p. 335 (originally published in Norwegian as *Edvard Grieg: Mennesket og kunstneren* (Oslo: Aschehoug, 1980)). The compositional genesis of the collection is also summarised in Schjelderup-Ebbe's '"Rett fra kua" – Edvard Griegs *19 norske folkeviser*, op. 66', *Studia Musicologica Norvegica*, 25 (1999), 9–11.

[21] Grieg, letter to Julius Röntgen, 22 August 1896 ('Allerdings habe ich haarreissende harmonische Kombinationen zu Papier gebracht. Zu meiner Entschuldigung sei aber gesagt, dass sie nicht am Klavier entstanden sind, sondern im Gehirn. Wenn man den Vöringfos unter sich hat, fühlt man sich unabhängiger und wagt mehr als unten im Thal'). *Edvard Grieg und Julius Röntgen: Briefwechsel 1883–1907*, ed. Finn Benestad and Hanna de Vries Stavland (Amsterdam: Koninklijke Vereniging voor Nederlandse Muziekgeschiedenis, 1997), p. 169.

Percy Grainger's later account of the composer appears to corroborate the mysterious connexion between nature and musical harmony Grieg felt in the mountains of Western Norway. The two works cited by Grainger, Nos 18 and 14 of the Op. 66 collection, are indeed the two most harmonically developed and impressionistic in sonority of the set.

It was a joy to see how uplifted he became high up in the hills. He told me he never felt that his harmonic flight was so daring and free as when he composed up on high, and how some of his very loveliest things – such as 'Jeg gaar i tusind tanker' – 'I walk with a thousand thoughts', 'I Ola Dalom' (Op. 66) – came to paper in little Saeter-huts up in the Jotunheim mountains.[22]

And the harmonic world Grieg glimpsed in nature might also be found via the human subjects that live among it – that quintessential Romantic category, the 'folk'. In a vein reminiscent of the letter to Finck, the composer, speaking more generally of Norwegian folksongs (and specifically of his recipient's own arrangements), writes to Agathe Backer-Grøndahl the year following Op. 66: 'How magnificent are these heroic ballads! It is as if the most profound harmonies lie latent within them, longing finally to come out again into the light of day.'[23]

As will be returned to at the end of this study, one might perceive a possible tension between Grieg's views on this question of nature and nationalism as manifested in musical harmony and the diversity of his practice, at least set against Germanocentric claims in music historiography. Put simply, the same appeal to nature is used both by a universalising German trend in music theory and by Grieg himself to oppose this hegemonic mainstream, while the very cultural relativism that resists such recourse to supposed natural laws as musical arbiter may well be the best way for offering some critical rehabilitation of Grieg's compositional significance. Indeed, much of the subsequent analytical account will be aimed at teasing out the implications this apparent contradiction possesses for the understanding of his music.

Aims of the Present Monograph

This present study, then, examines how the music of Grieg may deepen our understanding of the complexity and diversity of late-nineteenth-century harmonic practice. A central focus is provided by Op. 66 (1896), but the account extends more widely to cover his piano music from the years 1890–1905 – the *Lyric Pieces*, books V (1891), VI (1893), VII (1895), VIII (1896), IX (1898–9), and X (1901); the *Slåtter* (*Norwegian Peasant Dances*, 1902–3), *Stemninger* (*Moods*, 1901–5) – besides freely drawing on

[22] Percy Grainger, 'Personal Recollections of Grieg', *Musical Times*, 48/777 (November 1907), 720.

[23] Grieg, letter to Agathe Backer-Grøndahl, 28 May 1897 ('Hvor herlig er dog disse Kjæmpeviser! Det er som de dybeste Harmonier ligger latent i dem, længtende efter engang at komme for Dagens Lys'), in *Brev i utvalg 1862–1907*, ed. Finn Benestad, 2 vols. (Oslo: Aschehoug, 1998), vol. I, p. 232, translation modified from *Letters to Colleagues and Friends*, p. 293.

a number of works lying outside these limits such as the song cycle *Haugtussa*, Op. 67 (1895).[24] It seeks to uncover what might be termed a 'harmonic grammar' of Grieg's mature style: not just an inventory of his harmonic practices but, going one stage deeper, the hypothetical laws or underlying principles that might be at work behind their functional use. Building upon this is the important question as to what extent one might further speak of a harmonic syntax arising from the grammatical functions identified in Grieg's music.[25] In general, this study will move from the former towards the latter, as, more explicitly, it will move from examination of harmonic sonorities to their succession.

Although the primary focus of this monograph is on the music of Grieg insofar as it exemplifies wider theoretical and historiographical concerns in tonal harmony, such a study inevitably has more specific implications for Grieg scholarship. Indeed there is a continual mediation in the following pages between the claims of these larger theoretical objectives and a desire to analyse individual works in order to attain a deeper aesthetic appreciation of Grieg's music in its own right. This state of affairs should be welcome, as fuller recognition of this composer's importance and contribution to music history is long overdue.

Grieg's continued marginalisation in musicological circles is reflected in the current state of research into his music. Excluding more popular introductions to the composer's life, scholarship on Grieg has hardly been plentiful, with a particular dearth of research apparent within the English language. A substantial body of work naturally stems from Norwegian scholars, concentrating primarily on biographical and source studies, though in recent years a younger generation has moved onto wider political questions concerning national identity and appropriation, especially as relating to Norwegian folk music, and matters of performance.[26] German musicology has shown greater enter-

[24] The term 'late', prominent in this book's title, is being used primarily in a chronological sense to denote the concentration on Grieg's music from the 1890s onwards, rather than being intended to call up any broader connotative meaning such as nearness to death, esotericism, a fragmentary quality, etc. (though a certain 'untimeliness' might be posited of some of this work, especially the Op. 72 *Slåtter*). 'Mature' might also have been used, but this word has evolutionist connotations suggesting that Grieg's earlier music is inferior or less developed (a view I am not wanting to emphasise so strongly), and thus late is preferred here. On the more specific notion of 'late style' applied to Grieg (and the Op. 73 *Stemninger* in particular) see Daniel Grimley's forthcoming article, '"In the Mood": *Peer Gynt* and the Affective Landscapes of Grieg's *Stemninger*, op. 73', *19th-Century Music*, 40 (2016).

[25] I might therefore have entitled this book 'Towards a Harmonic Syntax' rather than merely 'Towards a Harmonic Grammar': that I did not reflects a desire to avoid undue expectations, despite the provisional 'towards'. Moreover, given that music does differ from verbal language in important respects, the application of such linguistic terms to music is arguably unhelpful if taken too rigidly. The term 'grammar' in my title should thus be understood in a broad and inclusive sense, one that may extend to questions of syntactic placement.

[26] For instance the original Norwegian edition of Benestad and Schjelderup-Ebbe's biography (the two also collaborated later on a study of the chamber music); five volumes

prise than that of its Anglo-Saxon cousins, including a recent thematic catalogue, a projected edition of Grieg's correspondence, and with a modest number of significant articles and monograph-length studies appearing at a pace that has discretely quickened in the last two decades.[27] Despite sympathetic earlier accounts of the composer by John Horton, and a small number of one-off studies, it has only been with Daniel Grimley's 2006 monograph that English-language scholarship has really been put on the map (though the retired American philosopher, William H. Halverson, has performed a valuable service in making several important Norwegian works available in translation).[28] The composer's harmonic language – the topic of the present study – has been the focus of a handful of previous studies, though such accounts have seldom gone beyond a simple cataloguing of harmonic traits to ask more fundamental questions about how these individual elements are meaningfully employed in conjunction and fit together into a system of tonal relations.[29] There remains much to be done on Grieg; the current study is a small, but I hope nonetheless valuable, step in this direction.

An important consideration worth keeping in mind throughout the following discussion is the practical issue of what the compositional problems facing composers in Grieg's time might have been (and arguably might still be). One of the most pertinent of these is the balancing act between harmonic richness and colour on the one hand and a control and logic of musical succession on the other. John Horton has astutely observed that Grieg's harmonic use suggests 'his determination to get away from the traditional relationships of tonic and dominant', in other words, to escape from the banality of cadential

of letters and the composer's diaries, all of which were edited by Benestad (some in collaboration with other authors); the work of Asbjørn Eriksen, Peer Findeisen, Nils Grinde, Harald Herresthal, Ståle Kleiberg, Lorents Aage Nagelhus; and the pianist Einar Steen-Nøkleberg's *Grieg på podiet: Til spillende fra en spillende* (Oslo: Solum Forlag, 1992; an English translation was published in 2007). A number of short articles have been regularly published in the journal *Studia Musicologica Norvegica*, and in recent years papers from the biennial International Edvard Grieg Society conferences have been made available online on the society's website.

[27] Dan Fog, Kirsti Grinde and Øyvind Norheim (eds.), *Edvard Grieg, Thematisch-Bibliographisches Werkverzeichnis* (Frankfurt, Leipzig, London and New York: Henry Litolffs Verlag/Peters, 2008); *Edvard Griegs Briefwechsel*, ed. Klaus Henning Oelmann (Egelsbach: Hänsel-Hohenhausen, 1994–); the work of Hella Brock, Patrick Dinslage, Birgit Goede, Hanspeter Krellmann, Ekkehard Kreft, Klaus Henning Oelmann, Heinrich Schwab and Jing-Mao Yang; and several volumes of conference proceedings from the *Deutsche Edvard-Grieg-Kongresse*.

[28] John Horton, *Grieg (The Master Musicians)* (London: Dent, 1974); in more recent decades book-length surveys have been produced by Beryl Foster and Sandra Jarrett on the songs and choral works and by Lionel Carley on the composer's visits to England and friendship with Delius.

[29] Kurt von Fischer's 1938 study forms a partial and honourable exception (despite the Swiss author's tangential concern with a notion of *nordländische Folklore* that looks mildly problematic today when set against the broader context of 1930s' German culture).

over-articulation.[30] The analysis above of Op. 66 No. 1 concurs with this understanding, identifying a strong, though long-deferred, plagal tendency that partially undermines the role of dominant functionality. Alongside this anti-functional tendency runs Grieg's love of colour and harmonic richness: the composer himself suggested to Finck that he was 'born chromatic'.[31]

Yet one can have too much of a good thing, even with harmony: complete compositional freedom is not always helpful. As Schoenberg sagely observed in his *Harmonielehre*, when everything is permitted – when any chord can connect to another (in Max Reger's famous dictum), and any apparent dissonance between melody and harmony be tolerated – how does the composer narrow down this range of almost infinite possibility? What note or chord should come next, how does one go about harmonising a melody when the very idea of harmonic and non-harmonic tones is being eroded by the emancipation of ever more dissonant vertical aggregates? Without wishing to become ideologically embroiled in what might easily become a narrative of dominion and control, the need for some sense of logical order and progression seems fairly innate in the human mind and our cognition of musical succession.[32]

The theorist Ernst Kurth saw clearly these dual tendencies in late-Romantic harmony and their concomitant dangers.[33] After Kurth, one might speak of a centrifugal tendency – the freedom of succession developing from the development of chromatic relations, the ever more delayed resolution of ever more dissonant *Spannungsakkorden* – needing to be counterbalanced by some equally potent centripetal order. As will be suggested presently, despite – indeed perhaps paradoxically stemming from – his often pronounced semitonal linear writing, several of the techniques Grieg develops may be read as forming ways of controlling chromaticism and curbing the otherwise unchecked centrifugal forces.

[30] John Horton, 'Musical Personality and Style', in Gerald Abraham (ed.), *Edvard Grieg: A Symposium* (London: Lindsay Drummond, 1948), p. 126.

[31] Grieg, letter to Finck, 17 July 1900 ('Ein Freund sagte mir einmal, dass ich "chromatisch geboren" sei'). *Artikler og taler*, p. 52 / *Letters to Colleagues and Friends*, p. 229.

[32] Cf. Arnold Schoenberg, *Theory of Harmony*, trans. Roy E. Carter (Berkeley: University of California Press, 1978), p. 329. A post-Enlightenment narrative of the subordination of nature through instrumental reason after Adorno and Horkheimer's diagnosis might be suggested, especially given the connexion that Adorno elsewhere posits with Schoenberg's later development of serialism. The theories of Fred Lerdahl and Ray Jackendoff appear to support the point above (see *A Generative Theory of Tonal Music* (Cambridge: MIT Press, 1983)), as does Tymoczko's subsequent reading of tonality.

[33] Ernst Kurth, *Romantische Harmonik und ihre Krise in Wagners 'Tristan'* (Bern: Paul Haupt, 1920). An English translation of selections from Kurth's major theoretical writings – including excerpts from this book – can also be found in *Selected Writings*, ed. and trans. Lee A. Rothfarb (Cambridge: Cambridge University Press, 1991).

Especially pertinent to Grieg's practice here is the role of extended triadic harmonies in his music, which occupies a middleground somewhere between these two antithetical forces. Kurth's younger colleague and follower at Bern, Kurt von Fischer, intimates this dual perspective in his often insightful 1938 account of Grieg's harmony. Here, it is argued, Grieg's colouristic construction of chords may contribute both to an intensification of tension through expressive chromatic alteration yet at the same time result in a functional relaxation that leads to more impressionistic harmonies. The following account thus starts from an examination of the construction of chords in their own right, moving gradually to a discussion of their succession.

1

Extending tonality: *Klang*, added-note harmonies and the emancipation of sonority

In 'My First Success', a late autobiographical sketch written for an American journal, Grieg relates a formative experience:

> Why not start by remembering the strangely mystical satisfaction of stretching my arms across the piano and discovering – not a melody. Far from it! No, it had to be a harmony. First a third, then a triad, then a four-note chord. And finally both hands helping – oh joy! – a five-note, ninth chord. When I discovered this, my rapture knew no bounds … Nothing subsequently has been able to intoxicate me like this. At the time I was about 5 years old.[1]

The significance of such a remark, given Grieg's propensity for stacking up thirds into chords of the ninth, eleventh, or even thirteenth in much of his later music, has hardly been missed on subsequent writers. David Monrad Johansen finds this comment 'extremely characteristic', Benestad and Schjelderup-Ebbe note that 'it seems symptomatic of Grieg's later development that it was not a melody but a chord – and quite a dissonant one – that gave him such great pleasure at that early age', while Ekkehard Kreft begins a historical survey of the development of Grieg's harmony with this same quotation.[2] Such a remark also seems revealing in that it is symptomatic of Grieg's privileging of harmony over counterpoint or even melody. Schjelderup-Ebbe has argued elsewhere that one of Grieg's characteristics, observable even in his earliest works, is this very 'preoccupation with harmony at the relative expense of melody'.[3] We might start then, like the young Grieg – or indeed

[1] Grieg, 'My First Success' (1903), original Norwegian draft ('Min første succes') in *Artikler og taler*, p. 12 ('Hvorfor ikke begynde med at mindes den forunderlig mystiske tilfredsstillelse ved at strække armene op mod klaveret og finde frem – ikke en melodi. Langtfra! Nej, det måtte være en harmoni. Først en terts, så en treklang, så en firklang. Og endelig begge hænderne tilhjælp til – o jubel! – en femklang, noneakkorden. Da jeg havde fundet denne ud, kjendte min henrykkelse ingen grændser … Ingen senere har kunnet beruse mig som denne. Jeg har dengang været omtrent 5 år gammel)'. A slightly different translation is given in *Edvard Grieg: Diaries, Articles, Speeches*, ed. and trans. Finn Benestad and William H. Halverson (Columbus, OH: Peer Gynt Press, 2001), p. 70.

[2] David Monrad Johansen, *Edvard Grieg*, trans. Madge Robertson (Princeton: Princeton University Press, 1938), p. 21; Benestad and Schjelderup-Ebbe, *Edvard Grieg*, pp. 23–4; Ekkehard Kreft, *Griegs Harmonik* (Frankfurt: Peter Lang, 2000), p. 17.

[3] Schjelderup-Ebbe, *Edvard Grieg, 1858–1867*, p. 21.

the opening of Op. 66's 'Kulokk' – with revelling in sonority for its own sake. For in contrast to a common reading of late-nineteenth-century music as being more concerned with polyphony (such as is suggested by Schoenberg), whereby altered harmonies are the accidental by-product of a web of chromatic lines, Grieg often appears pre-eminently concerned with vertical sonority, with *Klang* in its own right.

In a now elderly, though no less perceptive account of his piano music, Kathleen Dale notes Grieg's unerring skill in choice of register and spacing of chords.[4] As seen in Op. 66 No. 1, tone-colour, spacing and register seem alongside harmony to make up a vital element in Grieg's writing. W. Dean Sutcliffe has pertinently referred to this component of Grieg's writing as a 'culture of sound'.[5] In his detailed and indeed revelatory analysis of 'Klokkeklang' ('Bell Ringing') from the fifth book of *Lyric Pieces* (Op. 54 No. 6), Sutcliffe points to the role played by such concentration on sonority in Grieg's compositional technique and wider aesthetics. The harmonic saturation of this piece by the interval of the perfect fifth has important connotations for a broader compositional ideology that emphasises both nature and Grieg's Norwegian identity, placed in opposition to a perceived Germanic norm:

> 'Klokkeklang', by placing the fifth firmly at the foreground of the musical picture, suggests an attempt to break through to a more elemental expression of national identity. It is a national identity that does not depend on overt manifestations of folk style but is rather to be found in the essence of a sound.[6]

Neither is this belief in sound as the conveyor of a distinctive national essence confined to Grieg. In a separate context, James Hepokoski has written perceptively on the importance of *Klang* in Sibelius's mature compositional style – his long pedal points, those ostinati pulsating with latent energy, the differentiation of monolithic blocks of orchestral sound and glistening purity of high strings – defined as constituting a characteristically Nordic compositional trait (in opposition to an Austro-German mainstream).[7] More recently Daniel Grimley has elaborated on this theme in Grieg's music as well as that of other Scandinavian composers such as Berwald and Nielsen.[8] Hence, it is immediately evident that this quality of Grieg's music is historically bound up with powerful cultural connotations of nature and national identity similar to those raised earlier in relation to the harmonic system.

[4] Kathleen Dale, 'The Piano Music', in Gerald Abraham (ed.), *Edvard Grieg: A Symposium* (London: Lindsay Drummond, 1948), p. 53.

[5] W. Dean Sutcliffe, 'Grieg's Fifth: The Linguistic Battleground of "Klokkeklang"', *Musical Quarterly*, 80 (1996), 168.

[6] Ibid., 179–80.

[7] James Hepokoski, *Sibelius: Symphony No. 5* (Cambridge: Cambridge University Press, 1993).

[8] Grimley, *Grieg: Music, Landscape and Norwegian Identity*. Additionally see the same author's entry for Franz Berwald in *The New Grove Dictionary of Music and Musicians*, and *Carl Nielsen and the Idea of Modernism* (Woodbridge: Boydell, 2010).

Even laying the problematic connexion posited between sound and nation to one side for the moment, such associations might come perilously close to affirming the belief that Scandinavian music is ultimately peripheral: the concentration on the supposedly inessential parameter of colour only emphasises such music's status as exotic, marked with respect to an unmarked German norm. It gives us sensuous surface rather than abstract structural depth, defined by its secondary rather than primary properties. Nordic music might hence appear to focus on a vertical, static state of Being rather than a horizontal, dynamic process of Becoming as in the German mainstream (even the fluviatile name denotes dynamism).[9] No less problematic, at least since the middle of the last century, is the atavistic notion of regaining a primary sonic *Urklang* or the search for a spiritual *Heimat* (in the manner, say, of Heidegger). Yet such notions of sonic identity were nevertheless an ideological reality at this time and as such possess a certain historical validity. Whether or not the sonorities of Grieg's harmony are actually closer either to nature or to the essence of his native country – that a bare Norwegian fifth in the Op. 72 *Slåtter* is somehow purer, more 'perfect' than a decadent, chromatically embellished German one (or that contained within a sugary Danish seventh, as Grieg once remarked) – matters less than the fact that this cultural association is well established and as such part of his music's cultural meaning.[10]

Returning to technical matters, one of the primary ways in which Grieg's concern with harmonic sonority is musically realised is in his construction of acoustically consonant chords that go beyond the standard major and minor triads. In this, his practice is consistent with a common later nineteenth-century desire to enrich the basis of conventional harmony: adopting a Schoenbergian-sounding formulation, one might speak of him extending tonality by broadening the range of harmonic tones countenanced as consonant. Just as the seventh above the dominant was once considered a purely linear phenomenon, what formerly would have been considered dissonant suspensions in need of resolution now become accepted as harmonic entities in their own right. Much of the basis for this feature lies in Grieg's creation of tertian structures extending beyond the

[9] I elaborate on some of these issues in relation to the supposedly peripheral or exotic status of nineteenth-century Russian music in my article 'Temporality in Russian Music and the Notion of Development', *Music & Letters*, 94 (2013), 78–118.

[10] Sutcliffe cites a letter Grieg wrote from Copenhagen to Johan Halvorsen on 3 February 1900: 'Although I am out of the country, my thoughts revolve around Norway and Norwegians, about all our youthful pugnacity up there. Yes, it is like the music of hard triads compared to all the soft-sweet seventh chords down here. Up there it is a struggle for spiritual existence'. ('Mine Tanker kredser trods al Udlændighed bare om Norge og Nordmænd, om al vor unge Stridbarhed deroppe. Ja, den er som Musik af hårde Treklange sammenlignet med alle de blødsøde Septimakkorder hernede. Deroppe gjælder Kampen åndelig Eksistents'. *Brev*, vol. I, p. 364 / Sutcliffe, 'Grieg's Fifth', 166, translation modified.) It will be noted that Grieg was not exactly unpartial to using seventh chords (though then again, he also had considerable affection for Denmark).

triad, which have a close acoustic connexion with natural harmonic overtones and can be integrated easily into customary tonal practice.

Extra-triadic Sonorities: Theoretical Context

The easiest option for creating extra-triadic sonorities within a traditional tonal context is to extend the dominant function through stacking up tertiary harmonies on top of it. In Grieg's music this goes well beyond the customary use of the V^7 chord to V^9, V^{11} or even V^{13}. Examples of this practice are legion throughout his oeuvre. The English musicologist Frank Sawyer, in his 1890s account of Grieg's harmonic style, felt moved to note how great a use Grieg makes 'of the higher dominant discords, the 9th, 11th, and 13th'. 'Grieg seems pre-eminently among contemporary composers to feel them as part of the great dominant chord'.[11] Half a century later John Horton would similarly remark on how Grieg treats diatonic sevenths, ninths and elevenths as 'masses of sonority, apart from their meaning in context', dwelling on them 'with naïve delight'.[12] Conveniently when considering a composer whose first instinct was apparently to pick out a chord of the major ninth on the piano, we may note that for the German theorist Georg Capellen (1869–1934) the primal *Naturklang* was indeed formed by the ninth chord.[13] It is perhaps no coincidence that the analysis of Grieg's music formed a significant part of Capellen's attempted justification of his harmonic theory. As will be shown presently, Capellen's theories offer a useful contemporary perspective onto Grieg's harmony.

Functionally, the large-scale prolongation of V is ideally suited to a location within the centre of ternary structures: plenty of examples of this practice in Grieg will be found in the *Lyric Pieces,* where an initially simple dominant chord is successively laden with superimposed thirds. In other instances, Grieg may start a piece with a lengthy dominant prolongation. A good case in point is the fifth song of *Haugtussa,* 'Elsk' ('Love'), whose opening articulation of a D minor triad is recontextualised on the entry of the vocal part as the upper triad of a larger G^9 chord (Ex. 1.1). In the repetition of the opening phrase this tertiary structure is extended into a dominant eleventh. Typical of Grieg's style is how after this dreamlike, static opening the following bars revert to a more chromatic and directed harmonic idiom, making use of sequence

[11] Sawyer, 'The Tendencies of Modern Harmony', 65–6.

[12] Horton, 'Musical Personality and Style', p. 126.

[13] Georg Capellen, *Die musikalische Akustik als Grundlage der Harmonik und Melodik* (Leipzig: C.F. Kahnt Nachfolger, 1902), pp. 9–14; the author's theories are developed most fully in *Fortschrittliche Harmonie- und Melodielehre* (Leipzig: C.F. Kahnt Nachfolger, 1908). A good English-language introduction to Capellen's thought is contained in David W. Bernstein, 'Georg Capellen's Theory of Reduction: Radical Harmonic Theory at the Turn of the Twentieth Century', *Journal of Music Theory,* 37 (1993), 85–116.

Example 1.1 Grieg, 'Elsk', *Haugtussa*, Op. 67 No. 5

and chromatic linear descent to obtain the song's tonic of C by the end of the first verse.[14]

[14] Also compare the opening 'Prologue' from the *Reminiscences from Mountain and Fjord*, Op. 44, or 'Spring Showers', Op. 49 No. 6. Although I am here interpreting chords of the seventh and ninth, etc., as tertiary constructions (as Grieg's account of his childhood discovery of the ninth chord implies), such entities could also be viewed as built

Another straightforward use of extended dominant-functioning chords would be in cycles of fifths that articulate strong cadential progressions, where chains of secondary sevenths or ninths may resolve quite unproblematically in a conventional functional manner. A mild example is the fifth progression decorated by ninths seen in Op. 66's opening *Kulokk*; an extreme instance of a chain of dominant sevenths is found in 'Night Ride' from *Stemninger*, Op. 73 No. 3 (analysed later, Ex. 3.22), where the sheer length and uncompromising realisation of the cycle virtually breaks down the tonal function conventionally associated with this progression. Moving almost full circle, a similar, non-functional effect to that in Op. 73 No. 3 may be created more obviously by the exact reverse means – by avoiding the functional resolution of what, in terms of pitch-class content, would appear to be higher-order dominant chords. As the following example from the *Ballade*, Op. 24, demonstrates, by negating any projected functional quality in the second-inversion sevenths through their semitonal shifting up in parallel motion, Grieg is able to turn the chords into pure harmonic colour, a stream of sonorities (Ex. 1.2).[15]

At lower orders (sevenths, major ninths) the addition of harmonically consonant thirds to the dominant root is often relaxing in effect, but on increasing scale may conversely spill over to become tension-inducing. This attribute was discerned earlier by Ernst Kurth in *Romantische Harmonik*, who saw the excessive intensification of constructive forces (such as tertian-preserving harmonic structures) as ultimately leading to their destruction.[16] Even if (as is commonly the case in Grieg) the additional tertiary steps are drawn from a diatonic collection and thus are generally less dissonant than chromatic alterations, such superimposition inevitably leads to functional ambiguity. The pitches forming the seventh, ninth and eleventh over the dominant correspond to the subdominant in function (and hence, at least initially, contribute to a sense of possible relaxation), while the eleventh and thirteenth beyond this belong to the tonic realm. On reaching the fifteenth the functional implication reverts back to the dominant. A hypothetical stack of diatonic thirds forming a dominant thirteenth or fifteenth would thus contain all three notes associated with each of the three subdominant, tonic and dominant functions. While such overloading might appear to annul any functional purpose by an exact equilibrium of forces, the compositional underlining of the dominant root and (in practice) frequent absence of certain intervening third steps almost invariably creates a sense

from interlaced fifths. As here in 'Elsk', Grieg's usage occasionally supports this latter reading: other examples could be given by the central section of 'Klokkeklang', Op. 54 No. 6, or the delicious supertonic ninth in b. 7 of 'Peasant's Song', Op. 65 No. 2.

[15] Though speaking in a different context, Kathleen Dale's description of Grieg's use of parallel sevenths in Op. 66 Nos 2 and 4 seems perfectly suited to the present example: 'Instead of resolving these chords conventionally, the composer allowed them to melt into one another like the colours of the rainbow, momentarily dissolving the tonality and creating an atmosphere of vagueness' ('The Piano Music', p. 57).

[16] See Kurth, *Romantische Harmonik*, p. 311.

Example 1.2 Grieg, *Ballade*, Op. 24

of accumulating harmonic and functional tension over a fundamental dominant, requiring ever greater release. Following Daniel Harrison's Kurth-inspired formulation, one might speak of an imbalance of energies that are 'discharged' onto the ensuing tonic chord.[17]

A highly expressive example of this technique in Grieg's music is found in the in-tempo introduction to the first movement of the String Quartet in G minor, Op. 27 (Ex. 1.3). The thematic material consists of a terse ascending figure filling out the third from $\hat{5}$ to $\hat{7}$, which is subsequently extended to a $\hat{9}$ above the bass. In turn, this four-bar unit is shifted in diatonic sequence up the minor triad on

[17] Harrison, *Harmonic Function in Chromatic Music,* pp. 90–102. The paragraph above has been inspired to some extent by Harrison's productive reformulation of nineteenth-century functional theories. The simultaneous sounding of tonic pitches alongside the dominant in the more extreme manifestations of dominant elevenths or thirteenths might also suggest some temporal anticipation of the resolution within the tension chord itself, or a blurring of the cadential $^6_4$ and V. Paradoxically this premature gesture towards resolution may result in yet greater tension; the tonic itself can be heard as a dissonance – like the famous premature reprise in the *Eroica.*

the roots i, III and V.[18] On reaching V in b. 25 the bass checks its ascent while the upper voices pile thirds successively on top, composing out the diatonic thirds a^1–c^2–$e\flat^2$ (V^9), c^2–$e\flat^2$–g^2 (V^{11}) and (inverted) $e\flat^2$–g^2–$b\flat^2$ (V^{13}) over this ever-pulsating D pedal. The final stage in this highly constructivist conception is the expected attainment of the d^3 corresponding to a V^{15}, thus regaining the root's pitch through an entire, two-octave diatonic-third interval cycle – but having reached this, the music topples over not onto any resolution but rather an even greater textural emphasis of the dominant in bare fifths in preparation for the arrival of the first subject. There is an extraordinary sense of pent-up frustration created by Grieg's nervously reiterative syntax, the single-minded development of the rising third motive on multiple structural levels and the corresponding steady escalation of harmonic dissonance. These qualities are maintained by the arrival at b. 45 of the expected first theme, whose obsessive motivic repetitions seem set on tearing its very content to shreds.

A related procedure is sometimes followed in central sections of *Lyric Pieces*, where after a certain level of tertiary overloading the dominant root will momentarily shift through such accumulated harmonic tension to a colouristic, often third-related harmony (in true second-practice style), before the dominant is ultimately regained and its functional energy 'discharged' onto the tonic for the reprise of the piece's A section. Examples may be found in 'Illusion', Op. 57 No. 3, 'Thanks', Op. 62 No. 2, or in elaborate form, 'Notturno', Op. 54 No. 4.[19]

Example 1.3 Grieg, String Quartet in G minor, Op. 27, first movement

[18] A technique typical not only of Grieg (see its modified use in the first theme of the Piano Concerto, Op. 16) but also of celebrated 'Nordic' precedents by Gade and Mendelssohn.

[19] Precedent for this procedure might be found in the celebrated Ibsen setting 'En Svane', Op. 25 No. 2, an early work containing some characteristic extended triadic harmonies, whose central passage builds up seventh chords on triadic roots above a dominant pedal, resulting in an implied dominant thirteenth at its climax.

Example 1.3 (*Continued*)

Alternatively, pitches may be added to the *tonic* chord to create a richer, more sonorous referential entity. The primary difference in constructive principle from that governing the creation of dominant-functioning chords is that here any harmonic tension that might result in the chord being heard as excessively unstable (and thus unable to function as a plausible tonic) must be avoided. In practice, the sixth scale degree is the most common addition, at least in the major, as the minor seventh added to the major triad immediately creates a dominant-seventh sounding sonority which raises expectations of resolution, while the minor sixth and major seventh are quite dissonant (though the latter sonority is found frequently in Grieg's late *Slåtter*).[20] An example of the major added sixth has been noted already in Op. 66 No. 1, and in fact this set is particularly rich in examples (alongside the contemporaneous Op. 67 songs). The forms of the minor mode appear more flexible, perhaps reflecting the plurality of associated scale-forms. While an 'Aeolian' minor triad+$\natural\hat{7}$ {0,3,7,10} is common in some of his contemporaries, in Grieg's music the minor triad+$\flat\hat{6}$ {0,3,7,8} and especially minor triad+$\sharp\hat{6}$ {0,3,7,9} appear more frequently.[21]

An example may be found as early as the final piece of the *Poetic Tone Pictures*, Op. 3 No. 6, where a half-diminished E minor+$\sharp\hat{6}$ is used as an extended tonic substitute following a chromatically undercut perfect cadence (Ex. 1.4). The cadential $^6_4$ heard at the opening of bars 9 and 10 slips through chromatic voice leading (itself thematic, taken from a motive in the piece's second bar) directly to the tonic in b. 11, bypassing the expected V. As if resulting from this unsatisfactory cadential progression, the tonic in b. 11 materialises with an additional $c\sharp^1$ adding a touch of Romantic unfulfilment to the tonic chord – open enough as to invite continuation, consonant enough as to blend into an adequately stable tonic sonority. Probably as a consequence of this thwarted functional resolution, the cadential approach in the material's reprise (bb. 25ff) greatly extends the chromatic progression in the bass to arrive this time at V, and with it a satisfactory perfect cadence into b. 29, now without added sixth.[22]

[20] In Op. 72 the characteristic major seventh sound is admittedly most often a passing linear phenomenon, either the result of a melodically decorative $\sharp\hat{4}$ set against degree $\hat{5}$ in a tonic chord or arising from the desynchronised blurring of V harmony over I. A genuine tonic+$\sharp\hat{7}$ is prominent, however, in one of the discarded songs for *Haugtussa*, the setting of 'I Slåtten' ('In the Hayfield'), EG 152 No. 6 (1895).

[21] The former tetrachord is found often in Dvořák for instance; see my earlier account of this added-note practice in 'Modal four-note pitch collections in the music of Dvořák's American period', *Music Theory Spectrum*, 32 (2010), 44–59. Rare Griegian instances may be found in 'Melody', Op. 38 No. 3 (bb. 3–4 and 11–12) and the second of the two *Waltz Caprices*, Op. 37 (bb. 13–17).

[22] This elision of a cadential $^6_4$ directly onto the tonic is also found elsewhere in early Grieg, an instance being the finale of the Piano Sonata, Op. 7, where it strategically under-articulates a projected cadence in the middle of the first subject group (bb. 22–3); a true perfect cadence is realised only at the end of the section (bb. 39–40 and 43–4).

Example 1.4 Grieg, *Poetic Tone Pictures,* Op. 3 No. 6

In the minor-key introduction to the Violin Sonata No. 2 in G major, Op. 13, a similar half-diminished minor triad with added major sixth is used for the tonic chords that conclude the repetition of the opening phrase, bb. 8–9 (Ex. 1.5). Standing in for the plain G minor of bb. 3–4, the sonority again provides enough stability to be heard as a satisfactory resting point whilst still imbuing the music with a latent harmonic tension that may subsequently be drawn on. Here it leads into a more mobile, modulatory passage that effects a smooth transition into the appearance of the sonata's first subject sixteen bars later. In both the pieces above the additional note contributes a distinctive colour to the tonic chord, one which moreover has a functional outcome in motivating the ensuing harmonic course of the music. Without quite being heard yet as perfectly stable, the addition of this 'Dorian' or 'Tristan' sixth to the minor triad nevertheless blends into a wider conception of harmonic tonicity, a step towards the enlargement of the triad found in Grieg's later music.

Added-note tertian sonorities built on functional roots other than V or I are more flexible in their possibilities. Put briefly, a local harmony may be treated in context either as dominant or as tonic for the purposes of accruing additional, supra-triadic notes. Clearly, the more added pitches a harmonic entity takes on, the more ambiguous the identity of its functional root may become. A subdominant chord may add the sixth (as would a local-level tonic), thus corresponding quite conventionally to a secondary dominant seventh in first inversion, or add tertian pitches to create IV^7 or IV^9, blurring the distinction with

Example 1.5 Grieg, Violin Sonata No. 2 in G, Op. 13, first movement

the tonic (an ambiguity familiar from Rameau's *double emploi* of the *sixte ajoutée*).[23] Moreover, given such tetrachords' fairly equal division of the octave, efficient voice-leading options to similar chord-types are naturally plentiful, thus widening the range of related harmonic progressions and hence potentially downplaying first-practice functionality in favour of an extended chromatic second practice.[24]

[23] See Chapter 9 of Rameau's *Génération harmonique, ou Traité de musique théorique et pratique* (Paris: Prault fils, 1737), pp. 115–19.

[24] On tetrachordal voice leading see Adrian P. Childs, 'Moving Beyond Neo-Riemannian Triads: Exploring a Transformational Model for Seventh Chords', *Journal of Music Theory*, 42 (1998), 181–93, Edward Gollin, 'Some Aspects of Three-Dimensional

Extra-triadic Sonorities: Historical Context

Grieg's propensity for extending the triadic basis of individual harmonies by adding thirds has in fact a notable theoretical backdrop in nineteenth- and early-twentieth-century harmonic theory. Grieg's teacher at Leipzig, Moritz Hauptmann, famously derived the dominant seventh from a double root of chords V and vii.[25] Revealingly given his generally negative account of his tutors in Leipzig, Grieg later spoke with particular affection and regard for Hauptmann. 'Despite all his erudition' claimed Grieg, 'he represented for me the absolute non-scholastic. For him rules did not have meaning in themselves, but as an expression of nature's own laws'.[26]

Hauptmann's interpretation of third-related roots was importantly taken up by Hermann Helmholtz, who used it both to explain the chord of V^7 and for sevenths in general.[27] By extending the principle that permitted the relative consonance provided by the overlapping partials of two roots possessing common thirds, Helmholtz furthermore offered a possible derivation of the minor triad as in fact a four-note entity consisting of two superimposed triads a diatonic third apart. A minor, for instance, is formed from the two roots of a C major triad and the artificial A minor, which overlaps its third and fifth scale degrees. The relatively weak major third degree formed by the overtone of the fifth partial (C♯ above the A fundamental) is overcome by the stronger minor-third degree formed from the fundamental and second partial of the twinned root C.[28] Helmholtz's calculations of 'roughness' resulting from interference between overlapping partials point to this minor seventh as being little more discordant than thirds or sixths.[29] Such a composite four-note collection further corresponds precisely to

Tonnetze', *Journal of Music Theory*, 42 (1998), 195–206, Richard Bass, 'Half-Diminished Functions and Transformations in Late Romantic Music', *Music Theory Spectrum*, 23 (2001), 41–60, Cohn, *Audacious Euphony*, pp. 139–66, and especially concerning their geometric properties, Taylor, 'Modal four-note pitch collections', and Tymoczko's more recent formalising in 'The Generalized Tonnetz', *Journal of Music Theory*, 56 (2012), 1–52.

[25] Moritz Hauptmann, *The Nature of Harmony and Metre* (London: Swan Sonnenschein, 1888), pp. 55–64 (§§110–24).

[26] Grieg, 'My First Success' ('Trods al sin lærdom repræsenterede han for mig det absolut ikke-skolastiske. Hos ham betød reglerne ikke noget for sig selv, men et udtryk for naturens egne love'), *Artikler og taler*, p. 23 / *Diaries, Articles, Speeches*, pp. 81–2. I do not believe that Hauptmann was a significant influence on Grieg's harmonic practice, however; as is implicit in the following discussion there are significant differences between Hauptmann's theories and Grieg's usage, not least in the use of higher-order tertiary sonorities above the seventh as entities in their own right.

[27] Hermann von Helmholtz, *On the Sensations of Tone as a Physiological Basis for the Theory of Music*, trans. Alexander J. Ellis (New York: Dover, 1954), p. 341.

[28] Ibid., p. 294.

[29] Ibid., p. 342. Helmholtz, well-advisedly, argues that whereas 'roughness' can be objectively determined by natural harmonic properties, consonance and dissonance are merely aesthetic judgements that may change according to cultural and historical context.

an inversion of the major triad with added sixth.[30] Both of these points are significant in that the resulting added-note sonorities are the same as two of those commonly encountered in late-Romantic music as extended harmonies – the tertian extension of the dominant chord, and the major with added sixth (or its minor with minor seventh equivalent). The existence of such harmonic sonorities is furthermore explainable quite independently by the abstract, geometric properties of these chords, while the conception of tetrachords as twin-root entities foreshadows certain aspects of the dual-tonic complex formulated later in the twentieth century by Robert Bailey.[31]

While at the end of Grieg's life some theorists such as Schenker rejected the idea that genuine harmonic sonorities could be legitimately constructed out of stacking thirds ever higher, others such as Schoenberg granted that such chords were compositional reality, however acoustically problematic their derivation might seem.[32] And as we have seen, another contemporary, Georg Capellen, went so far as to hold that the major ninth formed the chord of nature, and granted acoustic privilege to extra-triadic, tertian constructions. A harmonic 'monist', Capellen sought to return to the acoustic reality of the harmonic series, arguing against the theorising of imaginary undertones by dualists such as Oettingen and Riemann. For Capellen, 'the major triad, seventh and ninth chord alone are true copies (objectifications) of nature', corresponding as they do to the first nine overtones of the harmonic series.[33] The minor triad, in contrast, is an artificial creation, formed following Helmholtz from a double root, containing an addi-

[30] On the general overlapping of triads through shared tones and further consideration of pentatonic scales and the major-key added sixth see ibid., pp. 257–9.

[31] This feature has been explored from the alternative 'geometrical' angle in my 'Modal four-note pitch collections'. On the dual-tonic complex, see Robert Bailey, 'An Analytical Study of the Sketches and Drafts', in *Richard Wagner: Prelude and Transfiguration from 'Tristan und Isolde' (Norton Critical Score)*, ed. Robert Bailey (New York: W.W. Norton, 1985); Christopher O. Lewis, *Tonal Coherence in Mahler's Ninth Symphony* (Ann Arbor: UMI Research Press, 1984); and the introduction and essays in Kinderman and Krebs, *The Second Practice of Nineteenth-Century Tonality*.

[32] Heinrich Schenker, *Harmony*, ed. Oswald Jones, trans. Elizabeth Mann Borgese (Chicago: University of Chicago Press, 1954), p. 190; Schoenberg, *Theory of Harmony*, pp. 345–6. Hauptmann, as with Schenker, sees the ninth as merely a suspension (*The Nature of Harmony and Metre*, §238, p. 131).

[33] Capellen, *Die musikalische Akustik*, p. 15. Capellen holds that it is the major seventh rather than the minor seventh that should be included, an admittedly debatable choice given the intermediary pitch of the seventh partial in the natural overtone series. Grieg's use of ninths is often flexible on the quality of the seventh according to diatonic context.

Although Capellen does not draw on this, there is another potential link here to the idea of nature in that earlier nineteenth-century accounts of natural resonances (such as waterfalls) often interpreted such sounds as formed from a major triad sounding a fifth above a fundamental root (i.e. a major ninth without the third). The pointedly Schopenhauerian language of the passage above should also not be missed; it is no coincidence that Ernst Kurth, a more famous proponent of Schopenhauerian energies in music, held Capellen in high regard (see Kurth's *Die Voraussetzungen der theoretischen*

tional 'silent' natural seventh.[34] It is thus reasonable for the author that multiple forms of this artificial minor scale exist. Extending the double root seen in Hauptmann and Helmholtz, Capellen even briefly posits the existence of *Tripelklänge*.[35] Agglomerations of thirds can be parsed into a smaller number of governing roots, sometimes with opposed functional implications. Such formulations are fairly logical outgrowths of Hauptmann's thinking concerning the diatonic thirds that fill out the fifths marking the three functions associated with a central tonic (e.g. d–F–a–C–e–G–b–D etc.). They also connect very well with the more recent theoretical contributions of Daniel Harrison, noted earlier.

As stated, Capellen explicitly draws on Grieg to support his theories, including a fitfully detailed and sometimes curious analysis of the first four books of the *Lyric Pieces* as an appendix to his 1904 *Die Freiheit oder Unfreiheit der Töne*.[36] While no attempt is being made here to suggest the composer shared the German's theoretical ideas, Grieg's practice certainly seems very much in sympathy with this harmonic tradition of Rameau, Hauptmann, Helmholtz and Capellen (with a possible nod to Schoenberg later), as opposed to the contrapuntal or *Stufen* line. As seen, Grieg will employ at times a similar rhetoric concerning the harmonic return to nature; there is the same focus on vertical sonority, the appeal to a natural *Klang*, yet with it a mild relativism that is manifested in the plurality of minor forms permitted and their interfusion with modal scales of older provenance.[37] An approach informed by such contemporaneous theoretical perspectives may be productive for a modern-day attempt at understanding Grieg's harmony more deeply.

The most sophisticated compositional realisation of such extended harmonies may be found in the works dating from the last decade or so of Grieg's creative life. Both the song cycle *Haugtussa* (*The Mountain Maid*), Op. 67 (composed in 1895 and published three years later) and the *19 Norwegian Folksongs*, Op. 66, composed and published in the two intervening years, feature numbers written in a particularly rich and

Harmonik und der tonalen Darstellungssysteme (Habilitationsschrift, University of Bern, 1913), pp. 17–18).

[34] Capellen, *Die musikalische Akustik*, pp. 54–60; also cf. pp. 33–6, which implicitly connects the minor tetrachord with the subdominant major added sixth.

[35] Ibid., pp. 37–8.

[36] Georg Capellen, *Die Freiheit oder Unfreiheit der Töne und Intervalle als Kriterium der Stimmführung nebst einem Anhang: Grieg-Analysen als Bestätigungsnachweis und Wegweiser der neuen Musiktheorie* (Leipzig: C.F. Kahnt Nachfolger, 1904).

[37] Moritz Hauptmann, for instance, even devises a 'major-minor' scale-form (his inverted derivation of the minor triad being purely mental rather than a speculatively objective property as in Oettingen and the earlier Riemann; see *The Nature of Harmony and Metre*, §§82–5, pp. 43–4). It was noted that the most common minor added-note form in Grieg is not the Aeolian natural-seventh form posited by Helmholtz and Capellen but rather the more dissonant half-diminished major sixth. Justification is easier from a geometric than dual-root acoustic perspective (cf. Taylor, 'Modal four-note pitch collections', 46–9), but may also be sought in this same flexibility between mode (i.e. a minor+$\hat{6}$ is a P-related major+$\hat{6}$).

sonorous idiom, arguably forming the highpoint of Grieg's 'impressionistic' development of harmonic *Klang*.[38] In stark contrast, the late *Slåtter*, Op. 72 (1902–3), present a far-more jagged, angular soundworld resulting now from the dissonant aggregation of basic consonant elements. If not 'expressionistic', they certainly develop a new 'primitivism' that would leave its mark on the twentieth century.

Added-note Harmonies and Voice Leading in *Haugtussa*, Op. 67

Haugtussa counts as Grieg's only song cycle and arguably his most important achievement in the realm of song (a genre at least as crucial for the composer as that of piano music). Arne Garborg's 1895 verse novel of the same name, written in the rural form of Norwegian termed *landsmål*, tells of a young herding girl Veslemøy, a sensitive figure who possesses an unusual ability to perceive the spirits that live unseen around the other country folk (hence her designation *Haugtussa* – more literally 'female hill spirit').[39] Following a failed love affair with a local boy (the narrative told in the song cycle), Veslemøy loses herself in the realm of the trolls, who entice her into the fabulous 'Blue Hill'; only at the end of the poem will she return back to the drabness of the real world. Grieg himself related he found the poetry 'so full of nature mysticism' that he could not resist setting it: he appears to have been inspired almost immediately following the work's publication, producing twelve settings within a matter of months (besides sketches for a number of others), from which he finally selected eight for his cycle.[40]

The cycle's opening song, 'Det syng' ('The Singing' or 'The Enticement'), forms a perfect opening into the use of extended tonality in late Grieg. 'Oh if you know the dream, and if you know the song,/You will retain the sounds' run the opening lines of Garborg's text.[41] The seductive power of nature spoken of in the poem – beckoning both the

[38] The term 'impressionist' is used on occasion throughout this study despite its possible ambiguities or lassitude. It refers broadly to any or all of the following properties: a certain studied vagueness or blurring in harmony and musical outline; a concentration on the sensuous impression of sound as an object of perception (which may be associated with nature and/or the suspension of linear temporality); musical features prefiguring the so-called impressionist practice of Debussy *et al.*

[39] The linguistic debates – between a Dano-Norwegian *riksmål* (or *bokmål*) and a constructed but purportedly more authentically Norwegian *landsmål* or *nynorsk* – are an important part of the background to *Haugtussa,* although a topic slightly extraneous to the current inquiry. A more extended account of Garborg's use of the Norwegian language can be found in Grimley, *Grieg: Music, Landscape and Norwegian Identity*, pp. 117–24; also see Beryl Foster, *The Songs of Edvard Grieg* (Aldershot: Scholar Press, 1990), pp. 186–208.

[40] Grieg, letter to August Winding, 19 June 1895, *Brev*, vol. II, p. 275. The compositional genesis of Grieg's cycle is analysed in James Massengale, '*Haugtussa*: from Garborg to Grieg', *Scandinavian Studies*, 53 (1981), 131–53; on the role of nature in this work see further Peer Findeisen, 'Naturmystik als Kern der Einheit von Ton und Wort in Griegs Liederzyklus *Haugtussa*, op. 67', *Studia Musicologica Norvegica*, 25 (1999), 124–43.

[41] 'Å veit du den Draum, og veit du den Song, / so vil du Tonarne gøyme'.

protagonist Veslemøy and the listener on into the enchanted realm of Griegian harmony – is a fitting correlate to the composer's own views on the mysterious attraction he felt towards nature's hidden harmonies. As Grimley puts it, 'the song becomes a more universalised expression of bewitchment, like the opening "Kulokk" of op. 66: it serves simultaneously as a threshold into an enchanted mountain nature realm and as the gateway to an inner psychological state of heightened sensory awareness'.[42]

Example 1.6 Grieg, 'Det syng', *Haugtussa*, Op. 67 No. 1

[42] Grimley, *Grieg: Music, Landscape and Norwegian Identity*, p. 128.

Example 1.6 *(Continued)*

The song's opening sonority, an arpeggiated added-note chord with fluttering trill calling to mind some nimble avian natural inhabitant, sets the tone for much of the piece (Ex. 1.6). Immediately repeated up an octave, the sound is left hanging in the air without any attempt at resolution, the concluding F major scale blurred through the sostenuto pedal, leaving a diatonic wash of sonority. Evidently these natural sounds have no need of conforming to the functional harmonic behaviour of human artifice. This initial chord can be analysed from multiple perspectives. Functionally, it could be interpreted as a ii^4_2 – a third-inversion seventh built on ii – or chord ii over a tonic pedal. Neither reading is wholly satisfactory: the former is an unprepared and unresolving inversion with the seventh in the bass, while the latter understanding is undermined by the prominence of the tonic in both bass and upper melodic voice, which thus appears to form an intrinsic part of the chord rather than an additional element accruing to it.[43] Alternatively, the chord can be read as a B♭ major added sixth (IV^{+6}) or, from a twin-root perspective, as a superimposition of B♭ (IV) and G minor (ii) triads. Both the latter understandings have their merits, especially given the similar use of overlapping non-functional harmonic entities later in the piece. It is perhaps unnecessary, though, to insist on a single harmonic interpretation: part of the characteristic quality of the chord is its blurring and hence potential ambiguity between tonic, supertonic and subdominant elements.

As a sonority emphasised in its own right, the chord possesses a certain flatward or relaxing tendency. The constituent scale degrees ($\hat{1}$, $\hat{3}$, $\hat{5}$, $\hat{6}$) may indeed be analysed as tending more to the subdominant than to the other functions: $\hat{1}$, $\hat{4}$ and $\hat{6}$ all belong to IV, while $\hat{1}$ relates additionally to I, and $\hat{2}$ to V. 'Det syng' thus begins with a colouristic opening out and simultaneously a kind of falling inwards into an interior, subdominant realm. While not perfectly stable, the equipoise of overlapping major and minor triads, comparatively consonant sonority and minimising of any dominant tensions is not exactly unstable either. The harmony does not seem to be leading us anywhere except perhaps inward to explore the strange fascination of its own sonorous depths.

This static quality is no sooner confirmed as it is shattered by the rude jolt created by the entrance of the singer with the first verse of Garborg's poem. The subdominant function of the opening chord seems ill-fitted to lead unceremoniously to the tonic without dominant intermediation, and the initial F major scale is counterbalanced by a forthright affirmation of F minor. In harmonic grammar, too, the next five bars operate far more conventionally, utilising firm fifth-progressions with functional sevenths to lead to a V^7/V secondary dominant (i–♮VI^7c–♯VI^7–$\mathrm{II}^{(7)}$). The one slight kink in the progression – the semitonal root

[43] In his earlier analysis Daniel Grimley similarly questions the extent to which the opening chord may be read functionally (ibid., p. 128).

motion from VI^7 to $\sharp VI^7$ in bb. 5–6 – is smoothed by the first chord's second inversion, producing clear bass movement in fifths. Shifted down so as to begin on iv, the passage is then repeated in sequence, thus leaving us expectantly on a dominant seventh of the home tonic. There now enters a tonic major passage that magically takes up and elaborates on the sensuous added-note sonorities of the piano's introductory bars, taking us with Garborg's protagonist up to the blue mountainside promised by nature.

If the preceding ten bars were directed by functional dominant-progressions, the *Poco più lento* by contrast goes out of its way to avoid them. The harmonisation of the melodic succession $\sharp\hat{7}$–$\hat{5}$ in the second half of b. 14, for instance, is underpinned not by V but by the alternative triad sharing these scale degrees, iii, functioning as a dominant-substitute.[44] On its return in b. 16 this supporting mediant harmony is blurred with the tonic to create a twin-root $I^{\sharp 7}$/iii^{+6} entity, negating any sense of an effective dominant. Fused with the added-note harmonies that predominate from b. 17 onwards the result is a dream-like, amorphous atmosphere free of strongly directed harmonic motion.

In place of conventional tonic-dominant articulation, Grieg alternates mediant and submediant triads, followed by shifting added sixths or sevenths expressive of tonic or subdominant functions. Just as we have seen the dominant being substituted for by iii, so in the first half of bb. 14–16 the tonic chord is replaced by vi, whose ersatz tonic quality is underscored by the F in the bass (the effect is unmistakably of a tonic added sixth, even though the $\hat{5}$ just heard in the anacrusis is technically no longer present). The inward-tending oscillation between vi and iii here replaces the more mundane alternation of I–V, shadowing this progression a third lower. In the passage that follows, tetrachordal added-note sonorities take over, effectively blending the twin roots hinted at in the preceding bars: the $I^{\sharp 7}$ chord fuses I with iii while ii^7 combines ii with IV, these harmonies being interspersed with subdominant or IV^7 (= IV+vi) sonorities. Nowhere in the entire passage are triads built on V or vii to be found.

In terms of melodic line, the pitch organisation suggests a governing F major triad with variable additional fourth note of $\hat{6}$ or $\hat{7}$. Up and down, like the enchanted silver spinning wheel in the text, the vocal line moves in its orbit around the pitches contained between $\hat{5}$ and $\hat{8}$ (with the occasional nod downwards to $\hat{3}$), while the harmonies in turn

[44] Another notable example of iii acting as V-substitute in Grieg is found at the final cadence of 'Notturno', Op. 54 No. 4. This technique is also related to the use of the augmented triad in place of the diatonic dominant in more chromatic or minor-key examples. We might well remember Horton's suggestion here that Grieg often seems to want to avoid V. Other favoured techniques include the use of plagal cadences, or those involving the minor dominant, which undercuts the functional force of the dominant by lowering the leading note (a characteristic example may be found in 'Peace of the Woods', Op. 71 No. 4).

circle around added-note chords built up from the same scale degrees. The ii^7 that increasingly becomes the focus of these harmonic oscillations is the same sonority as opened the song (and cycle), and will mark the climax of this central passage at b. 22, now explicitly heard as a return to and consequent clarification of the piano's initial gesture. Again, though, the music trails off into the rarefied ether, to be confronted by the mundane F minor realm that returns.

Only at the very end of the song is this opening figure offered any resolution. A descending tonic arpeggio elaborated with the crucial added-notes of $\hat{7}$ and $\hat{6}$, followed *pianissimo* by a functional perfect cadence, calls back one last time to this alternation of harmonic worlds, whilst finally offering an understated cadential articulation of the more alluring one. The paradigm thus set up in Grieg's song – the alternation between rhapsodic nature-dreaming and the stern rebuke of reality, between added-note construction and sober harmonic functionality – sets up a motive of the entire cycle. Like the dreamer Veslemøy and the unfolding of her tragic love tale, the eight songs of Grieg's cycle alternate between nature pictures and expressions of a more human passion, ending in the murmuring waters of Gjætle Brook as nature entices Veslemøy into its realm.[45]

This closing song, 'Ved Gjætle-Bekken' ('By Goat Brook'), is the culmination of the nature mysticism in this cycle and arguably the most consistent articulation of added-note harmonies in Grieg's music. While the added-note sonorities may on one level be explained pictorially in terms of a Kurthian natural *Klangfläche* – a sonic depiction of the murmuring waters of the brook spoken of in the opening line of the poem – the composer also uses them to articulate a sophisticated underlying structural progression.

The rippling figuration of the opening traces an added-note I^{+6}, a relaxed, gently subdominant-tending articulation of the tonic A major with a hint of the relative minor that forms one of the superimposed triads (Ex. 1.7a).[46] The arpeggiated figure rising out of the bass in the left hand adds a passing b to its A major harmony, thus filling out a pentatonic pitch collection. As seen, however, the major added sixth is also equivalent in pitch content to the Aeolian seventh on the relative minor, and Grieg seizes on this harmonic *Mehrdeutigkeit* and the hints of F♯ minor already present by shifting the bass down a minor third at b. 5, realising this alternative implication in

45 With the example of Schubert's *Die schöne Müllerin* forming a powerful generic precedent, Grieg's cycle has often been understood as ending with Veslemøy's death, though in the context of Garborg's larger narrative this proves not to be the case.

46 The sound of the tonic added sixth has been prominent throughout the cycle, often associated with naturalistic scene painting. One of the clearest instances may be found in the flourish that opens the third song, 'Blåbær-Li' ('Bilberry Slope'), and which returns repeatedly to punctuate its stanzas.

the opening harmony.[47] In common with the natural *Klangfläche* theorised by Kurth and Dahlhaus, the music moves without really moving; amid the unchanging bubbling waters a darker eddy becomes momentarily apparent.

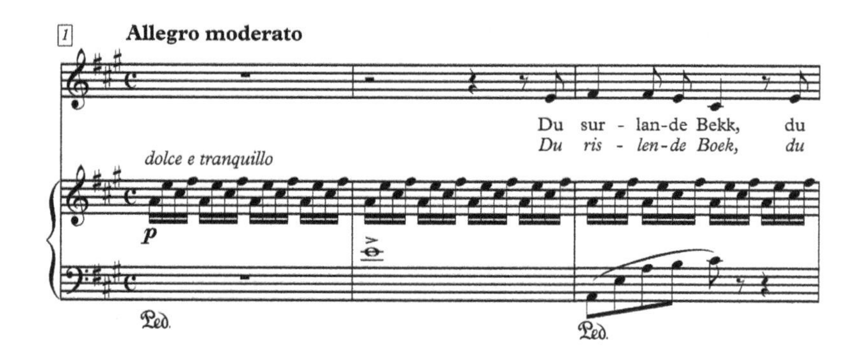

Example 1.7a Grieg, 'Ved Gjætle-Bekken', *Haugtussa,* Op. 67 No. 8

[47] For whatever reason, as Daniel Grimley has observed, this equivocation between tonic and relative minor seems particularly associated with A major. Other examples in Grieg include 'Dream Vision' Op. 62 No. 5 and 'In Ola-Dalom', Op. 66 No. 14 (both discussed below); an earlier precedent might be found in Schumann's 'Im wunderschönen Monat Mai' from *Dichterliebe.*

Example 1.7a (*Continued*)

The entire process is shifted now one degree higher, so that the $\text{I}^{+6}\rightarrow\text{vi}^{+7}$ progression becomes $\text{ii}^{+6}\rightarrow\text{vii}^{+7}$. With this diatonic shift, the mood darkens further as the relaxed major added sixth is replaced by a half-diminished seventh that suffuses its cooler expressive ardour over the music. Yet this harmony also forms an important escalation in the level of harmonic tension. If the opening sonority belonged to the tonic with a hint of the subdominant (I: $\hat{1}$, $\hat{3}$, $\hat{5}$; IV: $\hat{1}$, $\hat{6}$; V: $\hat{5}$), this new harmony moves significantly further in the direction of the dominant, dividing its constituent pitches equally between the subdominant already present ($\hat{4}$, $\hat{6}$) and dominant ($\hat{2}$, $\hat{7}$). As Harrison has suggested, the half-diminished $\text{vii}^{ø7}$ is a functionally mixed chord, depending for its ultimate effect on compositional decisions in spacing and doubling, and Grieg's lower-third shift for its second half to $\text{vii}^{ø7}$ has the consequence of moving the sonority's basis away from the subdominant realm (ii) and closer towards the dominant.[48] The prominent tritone now created in the bass (bb. 10–11), as well as the piquant a♯ passing note, only adds to the increase in harmonic tension that calls for some form of release.

The harmonic shift to a G^{9} chord at b. 13 ($\natural\text{VII}^{9}$) might seem initially to thwart such desires in typical Romantic fashion by a reversion even more flatward (IV/IV); yet this harmony is ultimately the stepping-stone for a strongly directed cycle-of-fifths progression aimed at the attainment of V.[49] Maintaining the extended tonal idiom of the song, every one of the following four chords is decorated by Grieg with added-notes: dominant ninths resolve to added-sixth chords, to be succeeded by the ensuing dominant ninth in the cycle (G^{9}–C^{+6}–$\text{F}\sharp^{9}$–$\text{Bm}^{+\natural6}$). The smooth voice leading between local V^{9} and I^{+6} chords – two pitches, $\hat{5}$ and $\hat{6}$, being held in common, rather than merely one as in pure triadic writing – should be noted here, as this same type of connexion will be systematically explored by Grieg in his setting of the second pair of stanzas.

On the arrival of the last harmony, v^{+6} of the expected V, the right-hand figuration trails off into the air, breaking the progression. There follows a moment of great expressive significance, as over a deep minor subdominant – the first purely triadic sonority in the entire song – the incessant rippling in the right hand falls silent and the carefully constructed functional progression breaks down. 'Ah, here I will rest' sings Veslemøy in an elaborated, though unfinished plagal close, the vocal line adding an expressive c♯² that momentarily creates a sonorous $\text{iv}^{\sharp7}$ added-harmony (surely heard as a dissonant appoggiatura here for once, although drawn out to expressive length by the fermata Grieg places over it). The repeated C♯–B–A melodic cadence in the accompaniment (bb. 19–20), while mirroring the piano's earlier echo of the vocal line in bb. 7 and 12, also surely calls back to the opening song of the cycle (the prominent upward gesture echoed between voice and piano in bb. 7–8 and 12–13). Now, however, the

[48] Harrison, *Harmonic Function in Chromatic Music*, pp. 64–72.

[49] As Dmitri Tymoczko has pointed out to me, this $\text{G}\#^{ø7}$–G^{7} progression is identical to the 'Tristan' voice leading – in fact corresponding precisely to the second 'Tristan chord' in Wagner's *Prelude*.

upward striving of 'Det syng' is balanced by a downward sigh at the cycle's close. Yet even by the end of the stanza, the harmony remains open on a iv^6_4. Not until the final strophe will Veslemøy find her rest. This same cadential figure will be returned to in every one of the ensuing four stanzas, in all but the final instance remaining unresolved.

To sum up, the opening strophe of 'Ved Gjætle-Bekken' contains an extremely subtle fusion of added-note sonorities and functional harmonic progressions. The pervasive extended harmonies are not merely decorative of a conventional functional structure but contribute through their own peculiar properties to a reworking of its deeper underlying principles. In such an idiom, moreover, the one moment of conventional triadic harmony stands out as a salient event. Just as witnessed earlier in Op. 66 No. 1, an opening linear sequence gives way to a strong fifth progression that seems set to arrive at a cadential articulation of the tonic, only for the latter to be undercut by a move to the subdominant. The replacement of structural perfect cadences by plagal ones is evident in both, as is the aching deferral of their promised closure to the very last bars of the piece. In both, the varied grammatical elements of Grieg's harmony are combined in a comparable syntagmatic order.

The rest of this song must be considered more briefly, though Grieg's creation would certainly recompense analytical attention beyond what is possible here. In overall structure Grieg's modified strophic design fits the second stanza of Garborg's poem to the music of the first, before recomposed third and fourth stanzas lead to the regaining of the opening music and tonality in the fifth and final verse. At the close, the plagal cadence implied and withheld at the end of each of the first four stanzas is finally achieved. This brief outline, however, passes over the extremely subtle way in which the setting of the fourth stanza's opening (b. 43) is already back 'home' on the $A^{+6}/F\sharp m^7$ added-note collection, while simultaneously estranged by the addition of a low B that turns the harmony into an alternation between B^{11} and $F\sharp m^7$ chords, entirely obscuring any sense of tonal return. Thus, it is not until b. 66 and the start of the last stanza that the listener is provided with a sense of homecoming and harmonic release.

Especially noteworthy is the manner in which Grieg maintains consistently tetrachordal harmonies throughout the song, while articulating in the third and fourth strophes a systematic yet flexible large-scale chromatic progression that plays on the efficient voice-leading possibilities between four-note collections (see Ex. 1.7b). In almost every case Grieg's modus operandi is to keep two pitches of the preceding tetrachord fixed while moving the other two downwards by chromatic step, but it is revealing how and when he alternates between the multiple possibilities for achieving such movement.

The third strophe starts off with a sequence of P* and R* transformations to the opening added-sixth tetrachord that maintain two and three common notes between chords respectively. This pattern gives way to alternating tetrachordal S* and P* operations, before finally articulating this downward shift between added-sixth chords

Example 1.7b Harmonic reduction of stanzas III and IV of 'Ved Gjætle-Bekken', Op. 67 No. 8: connecting lines show pitches retained across successive harmonies

via an intermediary chromatic tetrachord.[50] Though this chromatically altered harmonic sonority appears at the end of the stanza, the overriding harmonic soundworld is nevertheless of the added sixth. Chromatic chains of added-sixth chords are relatively under-examined in contemporary theory, but owing to the chord's multi-functionality – as major added sixth or minor seventh on a root a minor third below – this progression may also be conceived as alternating minor sevenths with major sevenths or chromatic tetrachords. Such seventh chords are still tricky to represent graphically, but an important aspect of Grieg's procedure may nonetheless be glimpsed by observing how the minor seventh chords comprising the odd-numbers in Grieg's sequence of tetrachords form the central pillars of the 'Power Towers' graphed by Jack Douthet and Peter Steinbach in their influential 1998 article (a modified version is given in Fig. 1.1).[51] Starting at position 8, Grieg's third

[50] The asterisk indicates a tetrachordal modification of the conventional triadic Neo-Riemannian operators P, R and S; the less familiar N indicates *Nebenverwandt*, following Richard Cohn's transformational development from Weitzmann, here given in a mixed triadic/tetrachordal form ('Square Dances with Cubes', *Journal of Music Theory*, 42 (1998), 290, developed in 'Weitzmann's Regions, My Cycles, and Douthett's Dancing Cubes', *Music Theory Spectrum*, 22 (2000), 98). It should be noted that the downward Slide* transformation applied to an added-sixth tetrachord enables the retention of two, not just one, common pitches between chords.

[51] Jack Douthett and Peter Steinbach, 'Parsimonious Graphs: A Study in Parsimony, Contextual Transformations, and Modes of Limited Transposition', *Journal of Music Theory*, 42 (1998), 256. I have rotated the clockface in Fig 1.1 so as to position 12 at the top, and slightly rearranged the towers' stories to correspond with the following graph (Fig 1.2), following the model of Richard Cohn. The large black circles at positions 2, 6 and 10 contain the pitches of their constituent diminished sevenths; each Power Tower forms an octatonic collection that gives the complement of the diminished seventh opposite it.

stanza cycles twice anticlockwise around positions 8–4–12–8–4–12 on the Power Towers cycle (F♯m^{7}–Dm^{7}–C♯m^{7}–Cm^{7}–Bm^{7}–A♯m^{7} [=B♭m^{7}]). The interposed even-numbered tetrachords form links (not shown on the graph) that differ by two chromatic steps from each minor seventh.

In contrast, after an opening that bides its time harmonically (the sense is of some deep-lying pre-dominant entity that will eventually spur on a purposive harmonic progression, which indeed reflects the V/V status of the opening B^{11}), the fourth strophe alternates between third-inversion dominant sevenths and half-diminished sevenths in descending chromatic sequence.[52] Such descending chromatic progressions using

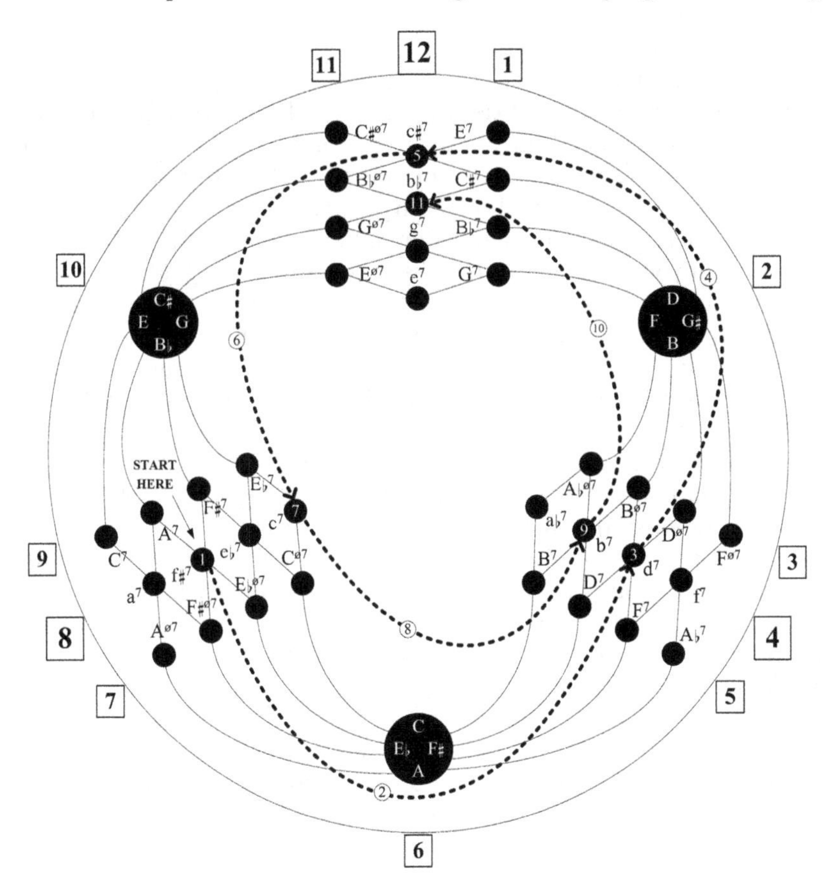

Figure 1.1 Tetrachordal voice-leading network for stanza III of 'Ved Gjætle-Bekken', Op. 67 No. 8, represented on Jack Douthet and Peter Steinbach's 'Power Towers' model

[52] The tetrachordal transformational operators S^{x} given below the chord progressions of Stanza IV in Ex. 1.7b are derived from the method developed by Childs in 'Moving Beyond Neo-Riemannian Triads', where 'S' refers to Similar movement in chromatic voices between tetrachords of Forte-Class 4–27 (easily confusable with the triadic S Slide or my tetrachordal S* Slide). The perplexed reader will be no doubt relieved to note that this labelling is not of great importance in the current context.

chains of 4–27 genus sevenths are more familiar in Romantic music and have received increasing scrutiny in Neo-Riemannian theory.[53] Stanza IV may again be shown as circling anticlockwise on the 'Power Towers' diagram, but this time through the odd numbers (starting from 7, through 5, 3, 1, 11 etc.). More clearly, though, it may be represented on Richard Cohn's derived Boretz spider/octatonic pool model: Fig 1.2 shows how Grieg's chain of harmonies circles smoothly round the three 'Boretz regions' of the 'Tristan-genus' tetrachord 4–27.[54] The one break in the progression is given by the use of a pure D minor triad at b. 60, which serves as the missing link between the B^7 of b. 59 and A^7 of b. 61 (the pitch A being held in common by all three chords).

Stanzas three and four, then, provide complementary ways of moving round tetrachordal cycles. Their syntactic principles are the same, but the harmonic entities they use – and most significantly their expressive effect – are quite distinct. The soundworld of Grieg's fourth stanza is qualitatively different from the third, the dominant sevenths implying an imminent functional purpose while their half-diminished cousins inflect a deeper note of Romantic *Sehnsucht*. 'Truly have you ever seen anyone so lonely as I?' asks Veslemøy, seeking now forgetfulness and oblivion in her own, more northerly Lethe. This alternation of seventh types resumes even after the statement of the inconclusive plagal cadence from the first strophe, given here at the original pitch of D but with an even more plangent $c\natural^2$–$b\flat^1$–a^1 vocal line. At length, the first – and only – appearance of a fully diminished seventh in the entire song (albeit over a sustained D–A subdominant fifth in the bass) creates a vii^{o7} dominant-substitute that effects the functional reattainment of the A added-sixth tonic for the final verse (b. 66).

'Ved Gjætle-Bekken' can be read as a systematic and highly sophisticated exploration of the possibilities of added-note harmonic writing, utilising principles drawn both from first-practice techniques in the opening stanza and from second-practice chromaticism in the third and fourth, besides demonstrating a structural control of harmonic articulation at the largest scale, all of which are accomplished through an original, extended tonal idiom. Added to this the expressive richness and beauty of Grieg's song and the surface allure of its nature-painting creates a remarkable piece, a fitting close to a collection he considered his finest achievement in the realm of song.[55]

[53] See for instance David Lewin, 'Cohn Functions', *Journal of Music Theory*, 40 (1996), 207–9, and the articles of Cohn, Douthet and Steinbach, Childs, Gollin, and Bass cited. Deeper discussion of this feature from a voice-leading perspective is given by Tymoczko in *A Geometry of Music*, pp. 284–302.

[54] For explanation of these terms see Cohn, *Audacious Euphony*, pp. 148–66 (extending ideas set out by Benjamin Boretz in 'Meta-Variations: Studies in the Foundations of Musical Thought' (PhD diss., Princeton University, 1970), and Douthett and Steinbach's 'Parsimonious Graphs').

[55] Grieg, letter to Torvald Lammers, 10 March 1898, *Brev*, vol. I, p. 488 / *Letters to Colleagues and Friends*, p. 464.

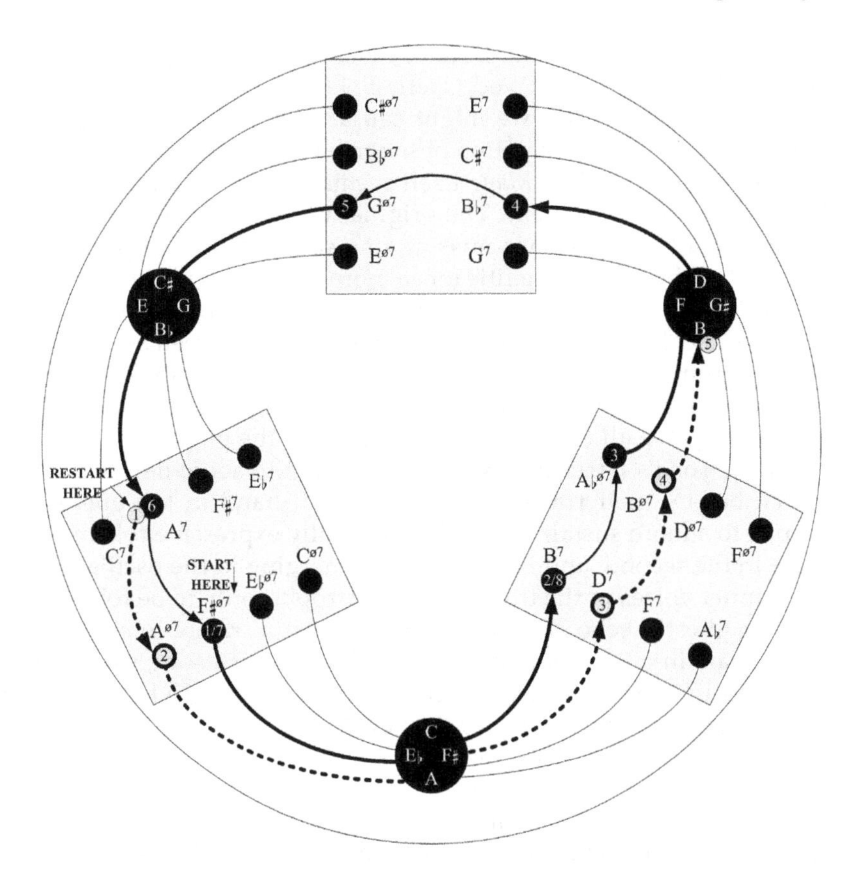

Figure 1.2 Tetrachordal voice-leading network for stanza IV of 'Ved Gjætle-Bekken', Op. 67 No. 8, represented on Richard Cohn's 'Boretz spider/octatonic pool' model as minimal displacements of perfectly even diminished sevenths

Extra-triadic Dreamworlds: *19 Norwegian Folksongs*, Op. 66

The exploration of sonority and added-note harmonies that distinguishes several of the songs in Op. 67 is reengaged in the contemporaneous Op. 66 set of folksong harmonisations for piano. We have already seen something of this quality in the account of the opening 'Kulokk' given at the start of this book. Indeed, as was explained earlier, this Op. 66 collection has long been considered a high-point of Grieg's harmonic imagination and inspired some of the composer's most notable statements on the connexion he perceived between the realms of harmony and nature. Particularly striking in their harmonic richness are the fourteenth and eighteenth pieces in this collection, as commentators ever since Percy Grainger have recognised.[56]

[56] John Horton, for instance, calls attention to just these two pieces, speaking of their 'exceptional interest on account of their extended scale, their fully developed pianistic

The first of these, 'I Ola-Dalom, i Ola-Kjønn' ('In Ola Valley, in Ola Lake') – a piece like 'Ved Gjætle-Bekken' set in 'an enchanted A major' – creates what we might call after both Schoenberg and Sutcliffe a type of 'emancipation of sonority'.[57] Even more than in the opening piece of the set, *Klang* itself seems here to become the fundamental aesthetic element. The original text for the folksong tells the tale of a boy who goes missing one summer day, presumably drowned in the lake of the title (once more enticed by nature into its realm). In vain his mother summons the church bells to be rung: she never sees her boy again. The villagers believe he has been bewitched and taken into the mountains. Again, as with 'Gjætle-Bekken' the piece's qualities of naturalistic scene-painting are immediately apparent. Above all else, Grieg's setting traces the poignant unfolding of the song's narrative through its changing sonic depiction of church bells – their transferral from the left hand in the opening strophe to a more sustained and harmonically expressive role in the treble in the second, and finally their submerging in the oscillations of the inner voices in the third and final strophe, only to be followed by their ghostly echo across the whole registral range in the very closing bars in a kind of benediction. This same folksong would be used later by Grieg's younger friend Frederick Delius in his orchestral tone-picture *On Hearing the First Cuckoo in Spring* (1912). Of note given the common tendency towards nature mysticism and its sonic realisation is how the bell sounds in Grieg's setting metamorphose into a bird call in Delius. Grainger fittingly speaks of both Grieg's and Delius's later settings of the melody as 'transcendental feats of emotional harmonization', 'uneclipsably lovely, resourceful, touching, sensitive'.[58]

If less systematic than that seen in 'Gjætle-Bekken', Grieg's use of extended tonal sonorities and their linear organisation is comparably expressive and in some ways even more impressionistic and dreamlike in 'Ola-Dalom' than the earlier song. The melody as transcribed by Beyer (Ex. 1.8a) is again almost entirely pentatonic with the solitary exception of the two Ds, the first treated by Grieg as an unaccented passing note, the other as an upper-neighbour. Its emphasis on $\hat{6}$ surely suggested the prominence of the subdominant in Grieg's setting, as much as the sense of an underlying four-note added-sixth collection {A, C♯, E, F♯} implied the ambiguity between the twin triadic roots of a tonic A major and relative F♯ minor (again, two features explored in

style, their outstanding beauty and their later influence on composers', *Grieg (The Master Musicians)*, p. 123.

[57] The apt term is Grimley's (*Grieg: Music, Landscape and Norwegian Identity*, p. 139). For an analysis of this piece on multiple levels that pays particular attention to the poetic and broader hermeneutic aspects see pp. 102–8.

[58] Percy Aldridge Grainger, 'About Delius', in Peter Warlock, *Frederick Delius* (London: Bodley Head, rev. edition 1952), p. 173. On the two settings see further Trevor Hold, 'Grieg, Delius, Grainger and a Norwegian Cuckoo', *Tempo*, 203 (1998), 11–20.

Op. 67 No. 8). The latter results in the reinterpretation of the melodic pitches against an F♯ minor (+♮7) backdrop in the second strophe of Grieg's setting, creating a ternary-type of structure with two verses of the melody based around an extended A major surrounding a more unstable and ultimately climactic central statement starting on an extended F♯ minor.

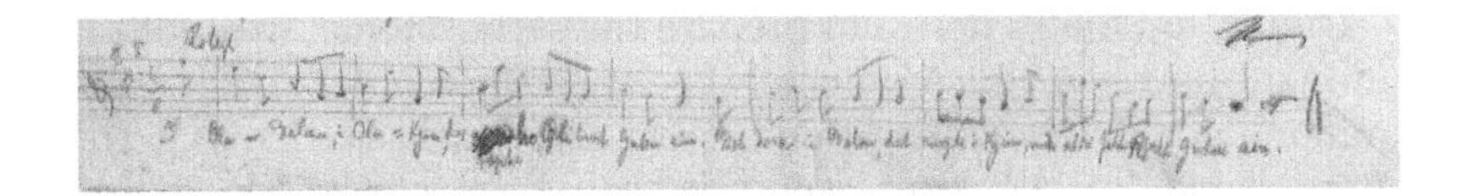

Example 1.8a 'In Ola-Dalom, I Ola-Kjønn', original transcription by Frants Beyer

The fundamental harmonic tensions of the piece, and the linear processes or paradigmatic models that they prompt, are created by Grieg's setting of the opening verse (Ex. 1.8b). A four-fold oscillation between I and IV$^{(7)}$ in the inner voices in the melody's first four bars opens inward again to a subdominant realm, the intermittent sevenths created by the melodic line's C♯ resulting in a comfortable equipoise between this subdominant chord and the tonic. All is stable here, save perhaps for the constant metric displacement of the bell fifths striking a faintly uneasy note. On reaching b. 7 the initial tonic of each pair of chords is altered to I$^{\natural 7}$, as if to lead more forcefully to the ensuing subdominant. Yet this latter harmony repeatedly fails to materialise. For three and a half bars the tonic seventh continues to chime on the first beat of every half bar, without any resolution to the subdominant forthcoming (the periodicity created with the bell fifths in the bass now suggests a comparably campanological quality to the inner voices, one less apparent when they had been harmonically mobile). In b. 9 a tenor d^1 creates a dissonant suspension that calls out even more strongly for the release of accumulated harmonic tension. Only at the very end of the phrase, though, does Grieg resolve his I$^{\natural 7}$ to IV, before immediately returning to $\hat{8}$ via ♯$\hat{7}$ in the last half bar of the melody, the latter underpinned by a reassuringly functional dominant. The simple, repetitive pentatonic melody has accrued increasing harmonic tension purely from Grieg's long-postponed resolution of the tonic seventh chord. Perhaps even more significant, though inconspicuous, is the linear model $\hat{8}$–♮$\hat{7}$–$\hat{6}$–♯$\hat{7}$–$\hat{8}$ set up in the alto voice in these opening bars, which runs in conjunction with the I–I$^{[\natural 7]}$–IV–V–I harmonic pattern. Itself a standard harmonic-contrapuntal schema familiar from the classical repertoire, it will become resourcefully reinterpreted within Grieg's extended harmonic setting.[59]

[59] Robert Gjerdingen labels it the 'Quiescenza'; see Gjerdingen, *Music in the Galant Style* (New York: Oxford University Press, 2007), pp. 181–95.

If the extended tonal qualities of the melody's opening harmonisation were understated, largely confined to $\hat{6}$ appoggiaturas and tonic sevenths, its effect residing as much in accumulated sonority and textural *Klang* as in extra-triadic harmony per se, the second statement is more sustained in its use of added-note chords. It is linked to the first section by a common-tone modulation (bb. 11–14) that sustains the pitch A held by both A major and F♯ minor chords.

Owing to Grieg's desire to prepare the second tonal area with its dominant, however, this A ironically becomes a momentary dissonance, a minor 'Chopin' sixth suspended over a C♯^{7} chord (bb. 13–14).[60] This central section's richer expressivity is created in part by the textural alteration in the setting, most notably the plangency of the sustained right-hand chords, but it arises most specifically from the harmonic intensification that runs alongside this new use of textural *Klang*. This development is based on a remarkably constructivist procedure: the overlapping at different pitch-levels of two statements of the $\hat{8}$–$\hat{7}$–$\hat{6}$ schema set up in the opening section.

From b. 16 the folk-tune is transferred into a tenor voice, still at its original pitch level. Below this, the baritone voices echo the minor thirds and harmonic content of the right-hand. The $\hat{8}$–$\hat{7}$–$\hat{6}$ schema, now transposed to F♯ minor, is moved into the bass voice, forming composite added-note chords in conjunction with the stable baritone part. Reflecting the varied chromatic inflection of the pitches forming $\hat{7}$ and $\hat{6}$ in the original model, this line now vacillates between ♮$\hat{7}$–♮$\hat{6}$ and ♯$\hat{7}$–♯$\hat{6}$ forms. From b. 17 until the attainment of $\hat{5}$ at b. 23 the bass shifts uneasily around the scale degrees of the paradigm set up in the first verse, $\hat{8}$–♮$\hat{7}$–♮$\hat{6}$–♯$\hat{6}$–♯$\hat{7}$–♯$\hat{6}$–♯$\hat{7}$–♯$\hat{6}$–$\hat{5}$. The result is an ever-shifting added-note quality, as the bass appends this variable fourth note to the F♯ minor harmony sustained in the upper voices.[61] Even more subtle is the way in which the bass's new pitch level suddenly and unexpectedly reveals a connexion with the motive contained in the melody's opening descent, F♯–E–D–C♯. Through its transposition to the relative minor in this central section, the schema that had appeared to arise as an inner voice merely through Grieg's harmonisation becomes relatable to the piece's original motivic source, the folksong.

Starting at b. 21, the pitches of the right-hand bells now follow down in suit, from a sustained A to an oscillation between G♯ and F♯. In fact,

[60] The term 'Chopin sixth' derives from the so-called 'Chopin chord', referring to the use of degree $\hat{3}$ as a suspension over a dominant seventh at cadences (especially characteristic of the aforenamed composer when this does not resolve by step to $\hat{2}$ but leaps directly to $\hat{1}$, as for instance at the close of the opening section of the Second Ballade, Op. 38). Some commentators describe this feature as a 'dominant thirteenth', but unless the ninth and eleventh are implied I prefer to see it as a unique lower-order chord of the dominant family, in order to distinguish it from the extended tertiary harmonies Grieg uses elsewhere.

[61] Kurt von Fischer also speaks of Grieg's technique of adding thirds *below* a given chord here (*Griegs Harmonik*, pp. 103–4).

Example 1.8b Grieg, 'I Ola-Dalom, i Ola-Kjønn', *19 Norwegian Folksongs*, Op. 66 No. 14

Example 1.8b (*Continued*)

this is nothing other than a new version of the $\hat{8}$–$\hat{7}$–$\hat{6}$ schema, heard at the original pitch level of A simultaneously with the bass's F♯ minor form. By b. 23 the bass schema has reached $\hat{5}$ and falls for the moment down to $\hat{1}$ as the melody comes to rest. There follows an extended passage of the most magical harmonic shifts beneath the ever-more clangorous tolling of the bells. This is undoubtedly the emotional heart of Grieg's setting.

To understand the import of this passage we must look to one further constructive principle governing harmonic succession that Grieg appears to have used in his setting: the retention, for long stretches, of common-tones between harmonies. In effect, for most of the piece either one or two notes form fixed pitches, around which the extended harmonies are constructed. For the opening section (bb. 1–12) the dyad {A, E} formed by the bells provides this stable basis (the A alone bridging over the transition in bb. 12–14). Bars 15–20 in the second verse retain the pitch A but replace E with F♯ in the tolling right-hand bells, thus allowing the section's harmonic recontextualisation of the folk-melody in F♯ minor. As both of these pitches drop out in b. 21 with the commencement of the expressively heightened G–F♯ oscillations, the C♯ held in common with the F♯ minor triad takes over. From b. 24 an E is added, the two pitches {C♯, E} persisting until the end of b. 27. Thus, until b. 28, the music has invariably sustained either one or (more commonly) two notes drawn from the underlying {A, C♯, E, F♯} A^{+6} tetrachord. What, distressingly, occurs at b. 28 is that this stable element finally disappears. The one thing left over from the preceding bars is merely the G♯–F♯ oscillation; the security provided by a stable element vanishes, replaced by the uncertain familiarity of a variable one. (The implications for a hermeneutic understanding of the piece, given its narrative of loss, could clearly be drawn out at length.)

The bass slowly shifts from a low F♯ to a prolonged B, over which the inner voices slip downwards chromatically, attaining the tonic pitch of A only at b. 32. Functionally, bb. 24–34 chart a cycle-of-fifths progression $F\sharp^{7}$–$B^{\sharp 7}_{4\,(\text{susp.})}$–$B^{\natural 7}_{3}$–$E^{4}_{2}$–[A]–$D^{6}_{4}$ that overshoots the projected A major tonic, trailing off (just as in 'Gjætle-Bekken') on an uncompleted plagal cadence. However, the expressive dissonances created by the falling chromatic inner voices against the G♯–F♯ oscillations and the use of inversion to minimise bass line motion considerably soften the effect, resulting in a miraculously suspended quality as the harmonies slowly sink ever deeper beneath the bells. At b. 32 the G♯ in the bells creates a wonderfully poignant dissonance against the low A of the D major $^{6}_{4}$ chord, following which the music falls silent.

For the third and final statement of the melody (bb. 34^{6}–42) the bells are silent, or at most we hear only their dim reverberation in the inner voices. With the return to an A major tonal centre Grieg's harmonisation resumes the simpler texture of the first section. Now the oscillations in the inner parts create richer passing harmonies: the alto line reiterates the $\sharp\hat{7}$–$\sharp\hat{6}$ movement of the schema (filling it in chromatically with a $\natural\hat{7}$ passing note in b. 38), while a tenor line, doubled in sevenths above, approaches the $\hat{6}$ scale degree from degree $\hat{5}$ below. After four bars the tonic pedal in the bass breaks off, as it slips down these very same pitches A–G♯–F♯. Once again a projected functional fifth progression II^{9-8-7}–V^{6}_{4} [–V–I] is undercut by an extended plagal iv–I close. The final masterstroke Grieg grants us is found in the penultimate chord, the modal $G\natural^{6}_{3}$ that leads up by step from minor subdominant to the ultimate tonic, a harmony whose effect reverberates long after the piece dies away in a distant peal of bells on an ethereal A major.

Throughout the piece the chromatic shading of the schema's pitches forming $\hat{7}$ and $\hat{6}$ has been variable. Initially, conforming to the classical paradigm, Grieg moves down via the flattened and up through the sharpened degrees. The second verse of the setting begins to confuse this neat functional sense, at first moving in conformity with the original model ($\hat{8}$–♮$\hat{7}$–♮$\hat{6}$–♯$\hat{6}$–♯$\hat{7}$) but presently hovering around the sharpened pitches (♯$\hat{7}$–♯$\hat{6}$–♯$\hat{7}$–♯$\hat{6}$–$\hat{5}$) in its F♯ minor line, while the overlapping A major line in the treble voices outlines the descending sharpened version ($\hat{8}$–♯$\hat{7}$–♯$\hat{6}$). For the third verse the sharpened version takes over in both alto and subsequent descending bass lines. The sustained minor subdominant in b. 42 continues the downward chromaticism introduced by the passing chromatic addition of ♮$\hat{7}$ in b. 38^3 and ♯$\hat{5}$ (enharmonic equivalent to ♭$\hat{6}$) in b. 39^1, pausing over the ♭$\hat{6}$ provided by the F♮ in the D minor chord. Rising up through the subdominant chord, Grieg's stroke of genius is to invert the model set up, reaching the tonic now through the ascending flattened version ♮$\hat{6}$–♮$\hat{7}$–$\hat{8}$.[62] This is the first and only time in the piece the flattened form of these scale degrees is heard ascending to the tonic – a kind of counterintuitive transcendence of expected functional behaviour, a moment of grace, as touching as it is inexplicable. With this transformation, the mournful a–g♯–f♯ of the bells' insistent chiming in the second verse is stilled by its inverse f♮–g♮–a progression.

In 'I Ola-Dalom, i Ola-Kjønn' we witness Grieg not merely exploring the role of textural *Klang* in order to create an impressionistic tone-picture from bell sonorities but furthermore constructing an extended tonal idiom from his inventive reinterpretation of a standard melodic schema. The continual presence of either the sixth or seventh scale degrees as an additional background pitch against the tonic triad relates once more to the added-note harmonies already utilised in *Haugtussa*, while the variability in their modal inflection suggests the important technique of scalar modulation, discussed in the following chapter. And not least in its captivatingly sonorous quality and expressive pathos, Grieg's conception fully justifies the praise accorded to it by Grainger.

Added-note harmonies are developed to a different end in the penultimate number of the Op. 66 collection, 'Jeg går i tusind tanker' ('I Wander Deep in Thought', No. 18). Unlike the novel directions in which the composer had taken harmonic schemes in Op. 67 and Op. 66 No. 14, in this piece Grieg seems pre-eminently concerned with enriching a conventional underlying harmonic syntax in a manner that sounds distinctly hymn-like in its opulent warmth. The original melody (Ex. 1.9a) conveys little of the harmonic potential Grieg evidently saw in this tune. Only the fermatas that mark the

[62] This rising ♮$\hat{6}$–♮$\hat{7}$–$\hat{8}$ cadential progression is found in a few other songs by the composer. A similar sound is obtained, for instance, at the close of each verse in 'Dereinst, Gedanke mein', Op. 48 No. 2 (1884), though there Grieg's setting is more clearly modal and progressive in tonal centre, starting with an oblique approach to the apparent tonic B major but ending in D# major. Perhaps even closer is the end of 'Farvel' ('Farewell'), Op. 59 No. 4, a work set again in A major.

end of its four-bar phrases might have called to mind the chorales Grieg would have set in his student days, along with their associated idiom.

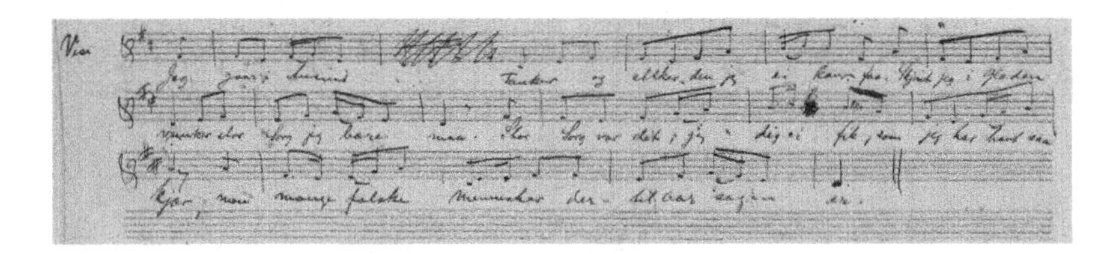

Example 1.9a 'Jeg går i tusind tanker', original transcription by Frants Beyer

The enriched tonality of Grieg's setting is evident especially in the texturally more developed second and third statements of the theme (the former is given in Ex. 1.9b). As pointed out in an earlier study, the harmonic background to almost every melodic note here is extra-triadic, achieved through the liberal incorporation of added-notes (the twin-tonic blurring of I and vi, the functional succession of seventh chords), linear suspensions and multiple appoggiaturas, as well as being softened through the incorporation of modal elements (especially the switch in the central part between major and minor).[63] 'I Wander Deep in Thought' is a fitting culmination of mainstream harmonic tendencies, expanded by Grieg into an immensely rich tonal palette of extended harmony.

Example 1.9b Grieg, 'Jeg går i tusind tanker', *19 Norwegian Folksongs*, Op. 66 No. 18, second stanza

[63] Taylor, 'Modal four-note pitch collections', 58.

Example 1.9b (*Continued*)

Stylised Folk Grammars: 17 Norwegian Peasant Dances (Slåtter), Op. 72

Quite contrasting in soundworld and expressive qualities are the *Slåtter* – Grieg's *17 Norwegian Peasant Dances*, Op. 72. Unlike the folk arrangements of Opp. 17 and 66, this set – often considered Grieg's most radical contribution to early twentieth-century musical style – is based on instrumental, not vocal sources, a repertoire of dances for the *Hardingfele* or Hardanger fiddle. A popular folk instrument in the West of Norway (the Hardanger region lies just south-east of Bergen, Grieg's birthplace), the *Hardingfele* is slightly smaller than the classical violin, with a flatter bridge enabling greater use of multiple stopping and its lowest string often tuned a tone higher (A–D–A–E). Most crucially, however, it possesses several sympathetic strings running underneath the four bowed ones, whose resonance gives rise to drone effects and complex harmonic interactions.

In the autumn of 1901 Grieg had been contacted by the Hardanger fiddler Knut Dahle (1834–1921) with a plea that the latter's repertoire be transcribed and hence preserved for posterity. The aging musician – who had learned his trade from famous nineteenth-century fiddlers such as Myllarguten (Torgeir Augundson) and Håvard Gibøen – was concerned that an entire tradition of folk music would disappear with him. This was not the first occasion that Dahle had tried to interest Grieg in the project, but this time, perhaps sensing age was not on their side, the composer acted swiftly, asking his colleague Johan Halvorsen (unlike Grieg, a violinist by training) to transcribe Dahle's repertoire. The result was a notated collection of peasant dances or *Slåtter* that piqued Grieg's imagination; although he remarked that it would be a 'sin' to arrange these pieces for piano, he confessed – rightly – that it was one he would scarcely be able to forgo.[64] Over the next year the composer worked on the seventeen arrangements that would be published in 1903 as the *Slåtter*. Disappointingly for Grieg, reception in Norway was relatively muted, but elsewhere this music began to attract a small but important following and in France the striking modernity of the set contributed to the composer's sudden heralding as 'le nouveau Grieg'.

There are many questions raised by Grieg's Op. 72, especially as relating to the appropriation of folk music, the tension between vernacular traditions and the concert hall, between the instrumental possibilities of the original fiddle source and those of the piano transcription, many of which have been the subject of scholarly scrutiny, even controversy,

[64] Grieg, letter to Johan Halvorsen, 6 December 1901, *Brev*, vol. I, p. 372 / *Letters to Colleagues and Friends*, p. 349.

in recent decades.[65] This notwithstanding, for the purposes of the current study we need merely note that the particular acoustic source of the *Slåtter* – the Hardanger fiddle – stimulated Grieg's thinking in ways not fully glimpsed in earlier music, and many of the corresponding differences in harmonic idiom – the preponderance of drones, use of bare fifths, sharply profiled melodic dissonances and complex overlapping harmonies – may plausibly be related to these origins.[66]

If the harmonic world of this opus seemingly stands quite apart from Grieg's earlier folk-music arrangements there nonetheless remain similarities with the techniques found in the *19 Norwegian Folksongs*. As the opening of the second, 'Jon Vestafes springdans', shows, the sense of consonant blurring between tonic and relative minor triads found throughout the added-sixth sonorities of Opp. 66 and 67 is retained as one element among several other harmonic techniques in the *Slåtter* (see the composite harmony on the first beat of bb. 3 and 4, Ex. 1.10). More characteristic, however, are the clearly delineated perfect fifths in both horizontal and vertical planes, the Lydian colouring of the Lombardic G♯ in b. 3 with the resulting accented clash of the major seventh with a dominant drone-pedal, and the radical desynchrony between the harmonic implications of different lines moving concurrently, the right-hand melody in b. 4² reverting to the dominant while the left hand remains on tonic harmony for a further beat.

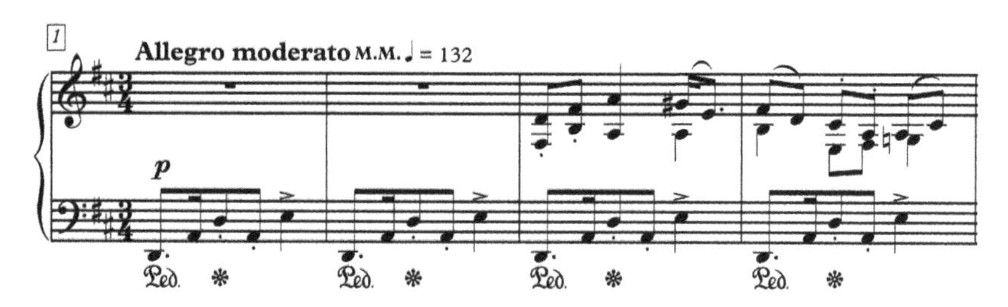

Example 1.10 Grieg, 'Jon Vestafe's springdans', *Slåtter*, Op. 72 No. 2, opening

A more extended illustration of the last technique may be found in 'The Goblins' Bridal Procession at Vossevangen', Op. 72 No. 14 (Ex. 1.11), which blurs triads expressing opposing functional implications at a length which goes beyond the soundworld of Op. 66. Following a rhapsodic, unmeasured opening, whose harmonic idiom suggests a curious mixture between modality and a chromaticism rare in this opus, the first phrase is formed from the six-fold statement of an unchanging

[65] A good English-language summary and development of these issues can be found in Grimley, *Grieg: Music, Landscape and Norwegian Identity*, pp. 147–91.

[66] It is worth noting that while Grieg was not directly involved with the transcription of the Op. 72 *Slåtter* he had certainly been exposed to the Hardanger fiddle tradition before; see Arne Bjørndal, 'Edvard Grieg og folkemusikken', in *Norsk folkemusikk* (Bergen: Nord- og Midhordland sogelag, 1952), pp. 285–316.

two-bar melodic unit in the right hand, under which the accompanying harmonies change every four bars. What is most remarkable, however, is that these harmonies themselves are out of phase between (and even at times within) right and left hands. From the upbeat to b. 4 the left hand continues to define the tonic function through its {G, D} fifth, strongly demarcating a two-octave registral space, while the melodic accompaniment lower in the right hand oscillates between ii and V, only reaching the tonic on the very last note of the unit. Such functional ambiguity is already inherent in the melody, which hovers around the extra-triadic degrees of $\hat{6}$ and $\hat{7}$ before settling finally onto $\hat{1}$. Thus while the bass is affirming the tonic, the upper parts simultaneously insist on pre-dominant and dominant functions.

As the bass fifths change to ii for the next four-bar unit, a new functional sharpness is brought to the right-hand harmonies, as if the previously blurred melodic object has swum into focus through synchronising the harmonic layers. With the shifting of the right hand's lower accompanimental figure in b. 9 so as to suggest ii^7, the harmonic clarification towards a clearly defined pre-dominant entity creates a strong impetus to cadential progression. Yet in the next four-bar unit (bb. 12–15) the process of correction goes too far, as the left hand elides the penultimate V-functioning vii with the final tonic resolution, a goal which is fully revealed only in its second bar. This overcorrection has the corollary that a projected sixteen-bar harmonic phrase (I–ii–V–I) is compressed into twelve.

In the 'Goblins' Wedding Procession' the multiple harmonic implications of the same melodic idea are thus realised through the successive rearrangements of its superimposed harmonies, a process of deepening harmonic perspective on the same object. (The implications for understanding the temporality of a musical nationalism that seeks the atavistic regaining of an enduring truth or essence through the renewal of a folk tradition are clear.) While going some way beyond Grieg's earlier practice, the blurring of triadic roots certainly recalls the 'impressionist' qualities of pieces such as 'Det syng' or 'I Ola-Dalom'. Yet despite the apparent clash of functional implications in Op. 72 there persists a strong underlying cadential progression controlling the succession of harmonies. The very end of the extract, meanwhile, further demonstrates the unusual scalar forms Grieg is moved to create in this set, the minor $\hat{6}$ of the $c\natural^3$ in b. 17 creating a surprise tonal clash against the $g\sharp^2$ major $\hat{3}$, implying an underlying 'harmonic major' scalar collection.

Notwithstanding the rhapsodic opening and superimposed triadic writing seen in the last example, Op. 72 in general presents a more angular side to the possibilities obtaining within an extended harmonic practice. Even one of the gentler pieces in the set, the third, 'Bridal March from Telemark', starts with piquant clashes created by a {f♯, g♯, a, b} cluster on the first beat of b. 2, created through the multiple ornamentation of degree $\hat{5}$ over tonic harmony (Ex. 1.12a).

Example 1.11 Grieg, 'Tussebrureferda på Vossevangen (Gangar)', *Slåtter*, Op. 72 No. 14

Example 1.12a Grieg, 'Bruremarsj fra Telemark', *Slåtter*, Op. 72 No. 3, bb. 1–3

In a continuation phrase (bb. 10–13), the harmonic recontextualisation of the melody over a first-inversion dominant creates an even more outlandish opening vertical formation of {g♮, g♯, a, b, c♯} (Ex. 1.12b).

Example 1.12b Grieg, 'Bruremarsj fra Telemark', *Slåtter,* Op. 72 No. 3, bb. 10–12

Such features led David Monrad Johansen to exclaim how, within this piece, 'we meet a harmony so bold and a leading of lines so ruthless in its uncontrollable impetus towards freedom that it seems on the point of bursting the tonal frame and starting out into atonality's anarchistic realm. And yet what colourful charm, what harmonic delicacy, even tenderness!'[67] Despite the fact that the vertical sonorities, taken by themselves, can be quite dissonant, Johansen is probably guilty of overstatement, in that even if atonality is foreshadowed in the level of harmonic dissonance and independence of lines, these lines themselves create a strong directional order and sense of tonal centricity. Both passages cited from Op. 72 No. 3 indeed lead to pronounced cycle-of-fifths motion that drives functionally to the attainment of dominant harmony. And while the piece's central, refrain-like idea (bb. 14–21) is underpinned by an unchanging ostinato pattern in the bass which seems immune to accommodating the melodic line above, the ostinato's trampling $\hat{8}$–$\hat{7}$–$\hat{6}$–$\hat{5}$ figure reinforces the underlying tonal ground in a more primitive manner (in both senses of the term).

In many ways it is most appropriate to view these pieces as forming a special subtype in the added-note *Klang* category. There is simultaneously both a new tonal simplicity (pedals; basic fifth progressions, even parallels; tonal ostinati) and yet a new overlayering of sonorities from these linear procedures set in motion against the melodic line,

[67] Johansen, *Edvard Grieg,* p. 349.

frequently resulting in quite dissonant clashes. As Sutcliffe pertinently comments, the *Slåtter* 'represent another firm renunciation of a mainstream harmonic practice. The harmonizations eschew an upholstery of thirds and sixths and, in attempting to lend idiomatic support to the tunes, emphasize fifths and the angularity of seconds and sevenths'.[68] Dag Schjelderup-Ebbe similarly speaks of 'hard and coarse' harmonic effects, where, the 'linear character of the dance music' results in Grieg consciously exploiting a style 'where blocks of sound clash with individual countermelodies in such sharp dimensions as minor seconds, major sevenths and tritones ... Unstable scales frequently produce cross relations, it even appearing at times as if two different keys are being used simultaneously'.[69]

Ståle Kleiberg sees the distinction between Grieg's earlier folksong arrangements and Op. 72 as being one between a mainstream harmonic language with Norwegian turns of phrase added and one where the deep structure is itself Norwegian.

> To introduce a linguistic analogy, we might say that what Grieg does [earlier] is to 'Norwegianize' a 'foreign-language' structure by adding characteristic traits from folk music to the surface structure. In op. 72 the facts are different. Here the application of the folk-music material is far more radical and more in keeping with its underlying structural principles.[70]

Kleiberg goes on to make the analogy between the two as comparable to that ongoing in contemporaneous language debates within Norway between a Norwegianised Danish (*riksmål*) and a more national, 'purer' synthesis of Norwegian dialects (*landsmål* or *nynorsk*). The idea is attractive, and certainly has useful implications for interpreting Grieg's music. Yet for all the surface roughness and deliberately coarse effects, underlying functional progressions may be found almost everywhere throughout these seventeen dances. Despite the constant cross rhythms, the Lydian fourth and the harmonic desynchronisation between hands, the functional I–vi–II–V progression opening No. 15, 'Skuldalsbrura' ('The Skuldal Bride'), is utterly transparent (Ex. 1.13), as for instance is the extended fifths progression in No. 6, 'Gangar etter Myllarguten' ('Myllarguten's Gangar'), bb. 10–15.[71]

To say that the deep structure of Grieg's harmonic language is qualitatively different in Op. 72 is debatable. Or, elaborating on the linguistic analogy, the vocabulary, and even perhaps grammar, does often appear quite different from much of Grieg's earlier music, as

[68] Sutcliffe, 'Grieg's Fifth', 167.

[69] Dag Schjelderup-Ebbe, CD liner notes to Edvard Grieg, Complete Piano Music (Geir Henning Braaten), vol. IX, Victoria VCD19033 (1993), p. 11.

[70] Ståle Kleiberg, 'Grieg's "Slåtter", Op. 72: Change of Musical Style or New Concept of Nationality?', *Journal of the Royal Musical Association*, 121 (1996), 49.

[71] Compare the latter example, too, with the similar procedure in Grieg's earlier 'Gangar', Op. 54 No. 2.

Example 1.13 Grieg, '"Skuldalsbrura" Gangar', *Slåtter*, Op. 72 No. 15

Kleiberg contends, but the underlying syntax, the concatenation of these new grammatical forms into longer statements, has much in common.

The drone-like pedals, ostinati and accumulation of complex non-diatonic harmonies found throughout this set are clearly suggested by the harmonic qualities of these dances' source instrument, the native *Hardingfele* with its sympathetic strings and non-classical tuning, but such techniques had already been a part of Grieg's practice and to this extent the new encounter with folk material just spurred the composer on to develop this aspect of his harmonic language further. Also shared with Grieg's earlier music is the focus on sonority. The impressionistic colouring of No. 14 has been noted with its quasi-modal opening and blurring of harmonic progressions. In the very first *Slåt*, 'Gibøens bruremarsj' ('Gibøen's Wedding March'), the use of sonority truly appears to have become a fundamental element in the construction of the music.

Following a four-fold statement of the opening march-theme that grows upwards both in dynamic and across the range of the keyboard, a contrasting middle section (bb. 19–30) prolongs the dominant A. From b. 30 a variant of the principal melody enters, sounding like a lead-back or preparation for an imminent reprise, over a new sonority in the bass, a mysterious *una corda* tremolo (Ex. 1.14).

Example 1.14 Grieg, 'Gibøens bruremarsj', *Slåtter,* Op. 72 No. 1

Example 1.14 (*Continued*)

Initially functional, sustaining a low dominant pedal against another line moving in parallel with the right-hand above, by b. 35 the tremolo settles down to an alternation between A and B that decorates the V pedal with the blur of its upper neighbour. At some stage now it may dawn on the listener that Grieg might be consciously imitating the sound of the *Hardingfele*'s sympathetic strings, transposing their slightly metallic whir into a novel piano sonority. As the dynamic flares up twice in the ensuing bars the sonorous power of this deep rumbling obviates any recognisable pitch content associated with the gesture. By the time the trill is taken up across the entire registral expanse from b. 46, colour has taken over as a constituent element in its own right.[72] Finally at bb. 50–1, all reverts back into functionality as the trill lowers the music by step down to the tonic for the (now fragmented) return of the opening march-theme that brings the piece to a quiet close.

Thus in this central section of Op. 72 No. 1, sonority itself becomes a salient motive, an emancipation of tone-colour as an integral element in the musical construction. The progression from functional harmonic behaviour to sonic sovereignty and back again articulates a curve suggestive of these pieces' barely suppressed nationalistic credentials, their location on the threshold between the laws given by custom and the unrestrained possibilities suggested to Grieg by folk music (one might say more broadly 'nature'), or indeed that between the harmonic traditions of the nineteenth century that lay behind him and the untrammelled freedom of the twentieth century ahead.

[72] The b^3 is the highest pitch in the piece, heard earlier at bb. 24–5 and 30. The trill's subsequent descent to D^1 in b. 51 passes through the previous lowest pitch, E^1, in b. 27.

2

Modality and scalar modulation

As several of the examples above have revealed, one particular way in which Grieg articulates the harmonic unfolding of his music is through the shifting between different added-note collections. Typically, this involves replacing one extra-triadic pitch and its characteristic sonority by another, such as is given by the shifts from major+added sixth to half-diminished or dominant sevenths across verses in 'Ved Gjætle-Bekken', or the alternating inflections of $\hat{6}$ and $\hat{7}$ in 'I Ola-Dalom' (with the varied added-note harmonies they produce). Such techniques constitute a small-set form of what Dmitri Tymoczko has designated 'scalar modulation' – the movement from one set of background pitches to another.[1] In traditional common-practice music a small number of pitches (normally three) go to form the type of vertical sonority characteristic of the music's harmonic soundworld, while a larger collection (normally numbering between five and seven) is used for melodic construction. Beyond such harmonic and scale sets lies the idea of macroharmony, which refers to the total number of different pitch-classes in harmonic use within a limited period of time. In simpler harmonic styles the macroharmony may be little more than the scale collection (with the addition, say, of the raised fourth degree or flattened seventh allowing modulation to V or IV), but in the highly chromatic idioms of late-Romantic music all twelve pitches may often be continually recycled.

What we saw happening increasingly in the music of Grieg is the expansion of harmonic sets of three pitches to those of four (sometimes indeed more). At any given moment in 'Jeg går i tusind tanker' the likelihood is that the listener will be hearing four different harmonic tones, a result of Grieg's extension of triadic harmonic practice towards the richer sonorities he favoured. The result is a blurring between traditional smaller sets of harmonic pitches and the larger scalar collections used by the melody: the 'A major' of 'I Ola-Dalom' is a mediation between a governing A major added sixth {A, C♯, E, F♯}, with its twin triadic roots of A major and F♯ minor, the melody's pentatonic scale collection, and new scalar collections formed from the additional inflected degrees $\hat{6}$ and $\hat{7}$.

[1] Tymoczko, *A Geometry of Music*, pp. 129ff. See also the same author's 'Scale Networks and Debussy', *Journal of Music Theory*, 48 (2004), 219–94.

Fig. 2.1 shows a hypothetical conceptualisation of the different set-types and hierarchies of pitch organisation in Grieg's Op. 66 No. 14. The twin roots of A and F♯ are visible to the left (F♯ slightly inset to reflect its subordinate quality in Grieg's usage): both could be conceived of as sets of cardinality 1. Over on the far right, under macroharmony, the table could ultimately extend to include all twelve chromatic pitches (though it is noteworthy that Grieg's extended harmonic practice largely ensures against total chromatic equivalency). Between the two extremes we find the pitch sets reflecting the customary sonorities heard in the piece. The primary difference in late Grieg from earlier music is that the balance is shifted towards the right, reflecting the larger set-sizes in use (alongside the bifurcated twin-root basis traceable back to the left). Indeed, we could regard Grieg's extended harmonic practice as blurring theoretical boundaries between the categories of harmonic and scalar set, concentrating the distribution of pitches into a medial stage between the two, from which a more extended range of harmonic pitches and a relatively limited range of melodic pitches are both drawn.

Pitch	Triad	↔	Extra-Triadic	↔	Scalar set	↔	Macroharmony
A	A major {A, C♯, E}						
			Harmonic Basis A major added-sixth {A, C♯, E, F♯}		Triad + variable, floating [♮/♯]$\hat{6}$ *or* [♮/♯]$\hat{7}$		
							Pentachord {A→E} + ♮$\hat{6}$ *and* ♯$\hat{6}$ *and* ♮$\hat{7}$ *and* ♯$\hat{7}$
					Melodic Basis Pentatonic melody {A, B, C♯, E, F♯}		
F♯	F♯ minor {F♯, A, C♯}						

Figure 2.1 Network of pitch collections and their hierarchies in 'I Ola-Dalom', Op. 66 No. 14

If the added-note harmonic basis of Grieg's late music is thought of as something lying between the traditional triadic and scale collections, the principle of scalar modulation becomes the natural extension of the alternation between added pitches observed in the different forms of the $\hat{8}$–$\hat{7}$–$\hat{6}$ 'Quiescenza' schema employed in Op. 66 No. 14. In other words, 'In Ola Valley' works towards a {A, [B,] C♯, [D,] E, F♯, G♯} scale collection in its second two strophes, only to be transcended by a {A, [B,] C♯, [D,] E, *F*♮, *G*♮} set at the very close. The particular form used there, featuring the retention of common pitches between scale collections (the A major triad), is designated by Tymoczko as a scalar 'subset' technique and is utilised by Grieg in other works.[2] This scalar principle offers a flexible way to contextualise hierarchical modes of pitch alteration in a piece. Following Schoenberg, one might even

2 Tymoczko, *A Geometry of Music*, p. 311.

envisage traditional modulation as taking place between different scale collections, for example C major → G major may be understood as based on an underlying modulation between the scale collections {C, D, E, F, G, A, B} → {C, D, E, F♯, G, A, B} with merely the inflection of the F♮/F♯ shifting.

Tymoczko reads a 'scalar tradition' within music history, which becomes prominent around the turn of the twentieth century in composers such as Debussy, but acknowledges that Grieg's music forms an even earlier example of such techniques.[3] In fact this aspect of Grieg's compositional style has been recognised for some time, albeit without any extensive theoretical underpinning. Dag Schjelderup-Ebbe comments on this same fluid interchangeability of different scale types in his early work on Grieg's harmonic practice, drawing attention particularly to the composer's borrowings from different modes.[4] Grieg himself was also quite aware of this feature. In a letter to Johan Halvorsen, the transcriber of the *Slåtter* melodies, Grieg speaks of his long fascination with the Lydian ♯$\hat{4}$ degree encountered within Norwegian folk dances, specifically the variable use of G♯/G♮ in D major. In particular, Grieg observes, a piece normally starts out with the sharpened, modal fourth degree, subsequently naturalising it towards its close. It will be apparent that this constitutes a mild form of scalar modulation.

> This 'peculiarity' you speak of with *G*♯ in D major was what drove me wild and crazy in 1871. Naturally I stole it at once ... This sound is something for scholars. The augmented fourth can also be heard in peasant song. It is a ghost from one or other of the old scales. But which one? It is incomprehensible that no one among us engages in musicological study of our national music...[5]

It is noteworthy that Grieg, even while professing his fascination with modal notes, seems theoretically unsure (and compositionally quite unconcerned) about the names of the modes used, albeit eager for future musicological research to explicate this matter. Thus, calling upon this opportune wish, we might do worse than explore the use of modality and scalar modulation in Grieg's music at greater length here.

The simplest type of scalar switch is the major to minor P-transformation, where the triad substitutes the minor for the major third (a {0,-1,0} operation) and the underlying scale collection does the same alongside its possible variants of $\hat{6}$ and $\hat{7}$ {0,0,-1,0,0,-1/0,-1/0} – an example which seems so ubiquitous in Romantic music as to require little further explication. One may note, however, how frequently

[3] Ibid., pp. 181–9 and 307ff, and 'Scale Networks and Debussy', 220 and 273–5.

[4] Schjelderup-Ebbe, *Edvard Grieg, 1858–1867*, pp. 169–70.

[5] 'Dette "mærkelige" som Du siger med *Gis* i D Dur var det som gjorde mig vild og gal i året 1871. Jeg stjal den naturligvis fluks [i mine "Folkelivsbilleder" [Op. 19]]. Denne Tone er Noget for Forskeren. Den forstørrede Kvart kan også høres i Bondens Sang. Det er Gjengangere fra en eller anden gammel Skala. Men hvilken? Ubegribeligt at Ingen hos os slår sig på national Musikforskning...' Grieg, letter to Halvorsen, 6 December 1901, *Brev*, vol. I, p. 372, translation modified from *Letters to Colleagues and Friends*, p. 349.

Grieg constructs the central section of a ternary design out of a close transformation of the outer material in contrasting mode.[6] A more extraordinary possibility of such scalar interactions, however, is witnessed in the second of the late *Four Psalms*, Op. 74 (1906), 'God's Son hath set me free', whose central section features the simultaneous presentation of major and minor modes across different voices. In a textural variation of the preceding verse, the baritone soloist retains the B$\flat$ major-key signature of the song's outer sections, while the accompanying choir changes to a sombre B$\flat$ minor. Though direct clashes between minor and major forms of $\hat{3}$ are avoided the result is nevertheless a curious fluidity of mode and constant wavering of $\flat\hat{6}$ against $\natural\hat{3}$. It is hard, in this, Grieg's final opus, not to think of a statement the composer made to Julius Röntgen a few years earlier on hearing of the death of a friend following a period of suffering: 'Poor Bosmans! Or lucky Bosmans! As one takes it. For life is just as strange as those folk-tunes, of which one does not know whether they were conceived in the major or the minor!'[7]

Yet the apparent self-evidence of these examples hides the fact that the minor mode actually consists of a plurality of scale types, reflecting the variable inflections of $\hat{6}$ and $\hat{7}$. More numerous, indeed, are the types of modulation that may be made between different minor scales. These problems of diversity are particularly evident in the minor since there exists no direct derivation from natural harmonic properties as persuasive as that which may be used to justify the major form of the triad and scale. Many theorists (especially those sceptical to the undertone derivation of the minor triad) saw the minor as inherently the result of human artifice: Capellen in fact holds in the existence of multiple forms of the minor scale stemming from its four-fold, artificial root.[8] Thus the minor mode is extremely close to earlier modality, from whence many theorists trace it.

As Ekkehard Kreft observes at length, Grieg was particularly taken with the minor mode, even more than most composers in the Romantic era.[9] A corollary of this is that Grieg's music may be prone to a wide variety of different 'diatonic' scalar sets without leaving major-minor tonality. Hence Grieg's practice simply opens up the plurality of sca-

[6] The technique is found for instance in the *Lyric Pieces* 'Scherzo' (Op. 54 No. 5), 'Vanished Days' (Op. 57 No. 1), 'Homesickness' (Op. 57 No. 6), 'Valse mélancolique' (Op. 68 No. 6); in the final 'Rigaudon' from the *Holberg Suite* and 'Night Ride', Op. 73 No. 3; in the concluding 'Temple Dance' from the *Olav Trygvason* scenes; and in numerous arrangements of folk material such as Op. 17 No. 5 ('Jølstring'), the *Slåt* 'Haugelåt Halling', Op. 72 No. 4, the third of the *Norwegian Dances* Op. 35, and the first and third of the *Symphonic Dances*, Op. 64.

[7] Letter of 22 August 1896 ('Armer Bosmans! Oder glücklicher Bosmans! Wie man es nimmt. Denn das Leben ist doch so sonderbar wie die Volksweisen, von welchen man nicht weiss, ob sie in Dur oder Moll gedacht sind!'), in *Edvard Grieg und Julius Röntgen: Briefwechsel*, p. 165.

[8] See Capellen, *Die Freiheit oder Unfreiheit der Töne*, p. 43.

[9] Kreft, *Griegs Harmonik*, pp. 239–60.

lar forms again, rather than restricting them, as was the case with the later eighteenth-century concentration on the major form as the central foundation of tonality. The fact that Grieg's justification may often be found in pre-tonal folk practice merely emphasises the contingent and localised (historically as well as geographically) nature of classical tonality. Again, in common with the historical and cultural relativism of theorists such as Helmholtz, any 'truth' in Grieg's nationalistic atavism might best be sought in its pluralism, its refusal to delimit tonality to one set of practices narrowly circumscribed by the major scale and a specific historical and cultural situation.

An early example of a straightforward switch between minor modes is found in the slow movement of the Piano Sonata in E minor, Op. 7 (Ex. 2.1). Here, the transfer from E harmonic minor to the Dorian mode is realised through the altered repetition of a one-bar unit.

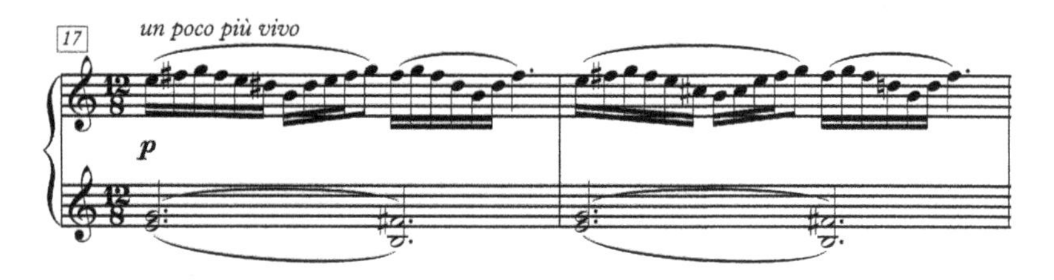

Example 2.1 Grieg, Piano Sonata in E minor, Op. 7, second movement

A similar alternation is given in the closing phrase of 'A Mother's Grief', Op. 15 No. 4, here between flattened (Aeolian or descending melodic minor) and sharpened (ascending melodic minor) forms of the variable minor degrees $\hat{6}$ and $\hat{7}$. Conversely, in the later 'Bådnlåt' ('Lullaby') from the *19 Norwegian Folksongs*, Op. 66 No. 15, the snaking thirds in the accompaniment articulate first raised then lowered versions of these pitches, in other words 'ascending' then 'descending' melodic minor scale-forms (Ex. 2.2). The initial minor/whole-tone tincture, alongside the parallel thirds, might call to mind the later practice of Sibelius.[10]

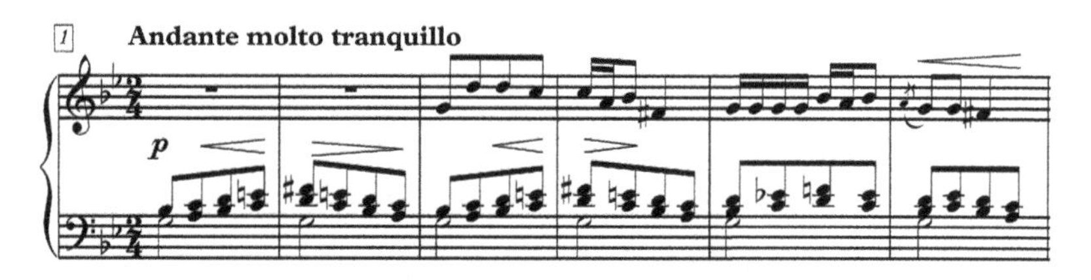

Example 2.2 Grieg, 'Bådnlåt', *19 Norwegian Folksongs*, Op. 66 No. 15

[10] See for instance the systematic procedures of scalar modulation in *Tapiola*, or the scale networks found in 'Metsälampi' ('Forest Lake'), No. 3 of the *5 Esquisses*, Op. 114. This matter is considered at greater length in a forthcoming study of mine, 'Monotonality and Scalar Modulation in Sibelius's *Tapiola*'.

A further simple instance of scalar modulation, this time involving the major, might be seen in the finale of the Piano Concerto in A minor, Op. 16, where the second subject famously appears in the closing bars with a prominent G♮ in place of G♯, in other words transformed from major to Mixolydian guise (a detail Grieg later claimed Liszt was transported by when in 1870 he played through the concerto in Rome).

It is especially in the works of the composer's last two decades, however, that scalar modulation takes on a more substantial role. One of the most extensive and finest examples of this procedure in Grieg's music is found in the *Lyric Piece* entitled 'Bækken' ('The Brook'), Op. 62 No. 4, which combines large-scale differentiation of scale collections with a strong suggestion of their associated added-note sonority. The piece articulates an expressive type of 'modulation' between an overriding 'Aeolian' minor+♮$\hat{6}$ tetrachord {B, D, F♯, G} and the 'Dorian' or half-diminished minor+♯$\hat{6}$ {B, D, F♯, G♯} encountered near the end. Though strictly speaking triadic writing prevails throughout, tetrachordal sonorities are present audibly through the constant flickering presence of scale degree $\hat{6}$ and use of the sostenuto pedal at the end.

Example 2.3a Grieg, 'The Brook', *Lyric Pieces*, bk. VII, Op. 62 No. 4, bb. 1–40

Example 2.3a *(Continued)*

Example 2.3a (*Continued*)

Example 2.3b Grieg, 'The Brook', *Lyric Pieces*, bk. VII, Op. 62 No. 4, bb. 65–81

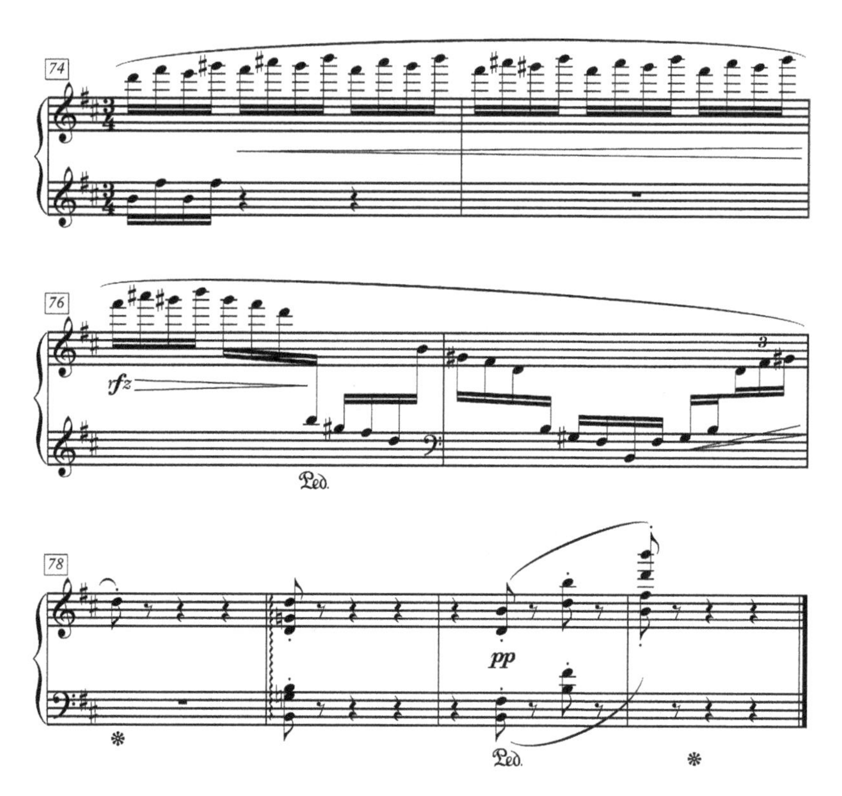

Example 2.3b (*Continued*)

The opening bars accustom us to the characteristic, rather bleak soundworld of this piece, with the rapid F♯–G♮ oscillations creating a blur of minor-$\hat{6}$ around the B minor triad (Ex. 2.3a). The Aeolian scalar basis is clarified in the next two bars with a descending variant of the broken-third figure that passes through A♮ and G♮ to F♯ (and beyond). Yet the bass's linear descent in bb. 5–8 immediately fills out this interval chromatically, passing through the major and minor forms of these two scale degrees (though the ♯$\hat{7}$, perhaps significantly, is notated by Grieg as ♭$\hat{8}$). Greater scalar dissonance is created in the following section (bb. 17ff), where an ascending sequence (Bm→C→Dm→E♭) produces grating false-relations between a descending Aeolian or melodic minor ♮$\hat{7}$–♮$\hat{6}$–$\hat{5}$ figure in the treble and the ascending harmonic minor leading-note motion ♯$\hat{7}$–$\hat{8}$ in the bass (bb. 17–18, 21–2). This tension is diffused through an elaborated version of the chromatic descent first heard in the bass in bb. 5–8, which now extends through an entire octave from g♭^{1} to f♯ (bb. 25–9), followed by the *harmonic* minor scale in broken figuration, which thus appears to have gained the upper hand over the Aeolian. Playing with the polyvalency of the idea of scalar interchange, Grieg now subjects the original motive to two different forms of scalar modulation. First, a 'tonal' transfer down three diatonic scale-steps creates a Lydian G version of the opening brooklet theme (b. 37). Then, subjecting this new Lydian flavour to 'real', chromatic modulation, Grieg gives us this same Lydian variant on the flat supertonic C♮ (b. 38), which, functioning as a Neapolitan, brings the music back to the tonic B minor (b. 40).

After a modified repetition of much of the preceding material, the closing bars of Grieg's haunting conception intensify the juxtaposition between different scalar bases, subjecting the piece's motivic material to an array of scalar operations (Ex. 2.3b). At b. 65 the ascending broken-third motive is subjected to a real, in place of tonal, sequence as its initial interval of a major third is systematically continued up by semitonal step. In effect, Grieg here replaces the diatonic scale with the chromatic scale as the governing measure of 'scalar distance'.[11] (The following minor sixths in b. 66 are formed as the inversion of this major third, as is made evident from their replacement by the latter in the immediate repetition of this two-bar unit in bb. 67–8.) The tensions between minor scale-forms that have been running under the surface throughout come to a head in the final stretto. Repeated plagal iv-i progressions pit harmonic minor ($\natural\hat{6}$, $\sharp\hat{7}$) and ascending melodic minor ($\sharp\hat{6}$, $\sharp\hat{7}$) scale-forms against each other, reaching an impassioned climax on the latter (b. 76), the music cascading down through its half-diminished minor+$\sharp\hat{6}$ subset (a touch of *Tristan* perhaps). The close is laconic: a dry, plagal iv–i. After the fluid ebb and flow between $\natural\hat{6}$ and $\sharp\hat{6}$ and the apparent final supremacy of the latter, the former has the last word after all.

As this brief account has revealed, the use of scalar modulation in 'The Brook' extends beyond minor and modal forms to the differentiation between diatonic and chromatic scale collections. The following number from the seventh set of *Lyric Pieces*, 'Drømmesyn' ('Phantom', or more literally 'Dream Vision'), Op. 62 No. 5, evinces if anything a more complex and sophisticated use of the scalar-subset technique in mediating between different major diatonic collections (Ex. 2.4).

The basic template of the opening section is clear enough: a simple four-bar melodic idea, given four times in varied form, descends after its second statement by chromatic step. This occurs over a bass that likewise descends by semitone, though here in contrast after its first and third statements. In voice-leading terms the melodic voice simply moves from F♯ to E through the intermediary chromatic degree, while across the same twenty bars the bass completes a larger chromatic descent from A to E. However, the precise relation between bass, melodic line, and underlying scale collection is much more complex in Grieg's musical realisation, resulting in a structural sophistication that belies the comparatively minimal material used.

[11] See Tymoczko, *A Geometry of Music*, p. 117. A similar technique of replacing diatonic by chromatic scale-step is found in the posthumously published 'Wild Dance' ('Dansen går'), EG 112, as discussed in Chapter 3.

Example 2.4 Grieg, 'Dream Vision', *Lyric Pieces,* bk. VII, Op. 62 No. 5

In a brief though illuminating analysis of this passage, Dmitri Tymoczko has observed how the entire opening section is in fact 'based on a progression that uses semitonal voice leading to connect familiar seventh chords … Unlike nineteenth-century composers, however, Grieg treats the chords as a skeleton to be fleshed out by diatonic scales'.[12] Significantly, the melodic repetitions of the four-bar idea are

[12] Tymoczko, *A Geometry of Music,* p. 314.

not exact but in fact subtly altered across each pair ('a chain of enharmonic echoes' as Grimley aptly puts it) as the bass reinterprets these pitches as forming another set of scale degrees belonging to a different (though overlapping) scale.[13] The result is a succession of five- and six-note pitch collections each connected to its neighbours by common tones, a complex variant of the scalar-subset modulation. For instance the first two phrases shift from the pitch-class set {A, C♯, E, F♯, G♯} to a {B♭, D♭, E♭, F, G♭, A♭} collection, three pitches {C♯=D♭, F♯=G♭, G♯=A♭) being held in common while one moves up efficiently by semitone and the other splits chromatically into two (see Fig. 2.2). With the shift in the bass line the music effectively undergoes a scalar modulation from a melodic idea starting on $\hat{6}$ in an extended A major to one on $\flat\hat{7}$ outlining $V^{7/9}$ over a tonic pedal in Mixolydian A♭. From this perspective Tymoczko has plausibly suggested that Grieg's opening section may be best heard as forming a succession of melodic entries on $\hat{6}$ in A major, $\hat{7}$ in A♭ Mixolydian, $\hat{6}$ in A♭ Dorian, and $\hat{7}$ in G Mixolydian.[14]

A final example in this brief discussion of scalar modulation in Grieg is provided by 'Ho vesle Astri vor' ('Little Astrid'), Op. 66 No. 16, which demonstrates how scalar ambiguity can become, as it were, the 'story' of a piece (Ex. 2.5).

Bars	2–5	6–9	10–13	14–17
Pitches				C
			C♭	
		B♭		
	A			A
	G♯	A♭	A♭	
				G
	F♯	G♭	G♭	
		F	F	F
	E			E
		E♭	E♭	
				D
	C♯	D♭		

Figure 2.2 Pitch-class overlap between successive scale collections in Grieg's 'Dream Vision', Op. 62 No. 5

[13] Grimley, *Grieg: Music, Landscape and Norwegian Identity*, p. 142. As Tymoczko notes, Grieg's conception contains 'an extremely subtle counterpoint between the scale, tonic and melody, in which the three elements never once move in parallel' (*A Geometry of Music*, p. 314).

[14] Tymoczko, *A Geometry of Music*, p. 316. The origins of this procedure probably lie in the favoured second-practice technique of common-tone reinterpretation; a revealing precursor of this passage can be found in the central *Poco meno Allegro* section of the *Waltz Caprice* Op. 37 No. 2, where the pitch B (alongside its lower chromatic neighbour A#) is successively reinterpreted in the harmonic contexts of E, A⁹, G#m, G, Bm, B°, and B (bb. 54–85; a process extended in the following bars).

Example 2.5 Grieg, 'Ho vesle Astri vor', *19 Norwegian Folksongs*, Op. 66 No. 16

Example 2.5 (*Continued*)

Here, the entire setting revolves around a missing ficta, D♯, and the witty conflict that ensues between D♮ and D♯ with their associated scalar modes. The opening fifths B–E would most obviously suggest an E major tonic, but while the melodic idea that enters on the upbeat to b. 3 could well be in E (the accompaniment even implies a repeated V–I cadence), the leading-note D remains resolutely flattened. At length the listener probably decides on a modal Mixolydian E as forming the most plausible key. Yet now, after the four-fold reiteration of the 'modal' B–D♮–E ($\hat{5}$–♮$\hat{7}$–$\hat{8}$) motive, a linear descent in the accompanimental voices leads to a strong perfect cadence in A (bb. 7–10). Evidently the entire phrase had begun on the dominant, the B–E oscillations in bb. 3–6 forming the start of a large ii–V–I cadence leading to the attainment of the tonic at the end. We are not in a Mixolydian E after all, but just a tonal A major.

Now of course, no sooner has everything been clarified than the D♯, which had appeared to be missing – wrongly, it transpired – materialises (b. 11). The supporting harmony is changed momentarily to C♯ minor, but the alternating D♯/D♮ ficta colours the ensuing bars even when the music moves back to A major regions. Playful repetitions of material from bb. 11 and 7 spin the music out at length, a continual blurring of E dominant and A tonic being present not only through the D♯/♮ alternation but moreover from the prominent melodic focus on the G♯ leading note, even when given over A major harmony. A linear decent leads to a strong E^7 at b. 26, but the music teasingly overshoots the tonic, moving too far to the subdominant side. By now the course of the music is getting ominously darker, the harmonic horseplay leading more aggressively through the non-functional progression of bb. 29–31 as prominent tritones infiltrate the texture. Even after the tonic has once again been prepared by the E^9 of b. 31^2, the melodic line, set against an A major added-note collection, eschews clear tonic definition, while left-hand fifths try in vain to consolidate the A major tonality without the functional authority provided by the dominant. D♯s and D♮s are sprinkled liberally throughout. Eventually D♮ appears to triumph, with a subdued added-note sonority in bb. 39–40 forming a type of plagal close. Yet this relative calm is short-lived, as the warning tremolo is repeated, now with the missing ♯$\hat{4}$, D♯, which explodes in naked tritones across the whole texture. The D♯ that had seemingly been held at bay in the opening section can no longer be repressed; like a mischievous child, it has the last laugh.[15] Even the final perfect cadence

[15] Admittedly the song's text is not directly relatable to this musical interpretation. It speaks of 'sweet little Astrid', a beautiful girl who captivates a youth from Hallingdal. Though he has a lot going for him, Astrid can take her pick of men such as Rautroja or Gullvesto, and dance instead with them. In response the youth eyes up other possibilities, ending with the veiled warning 'Oh my dear girls … If you won't let me in, I will use my skill/and go down through the chimney, all on my long rod' ('Aa kjære mine Jentor … /slep eg? kje inn om Døren, så bruker eg min Konst,/å nerigjenom Ljoren alt på min lange Stang'). The text can be found in the Bergen Public Library in an undated

is decorated with D♯ as an acciaccatura to $\hat{5}$. Perhaps 'Little Astrid' was in A Lydian all along.

* * *

The concept of scalar modulation is a useful tool in understanding Grieg's manipulation of the inflection of individual pitches and the shifting from one set of background pitches to another, related one, which underlies such practice. Moreover, the implications of this technique extend well beyond Grieg's music to encompass a wider range of work from the early twentieth century. Tymoczko has drawn attention to this scalar principle in the music of such later composers as Debussy, Ravel, Janáček, Prokofiev and Shostakovich, but the idea of scalar modulation might also be applied with significant, even revelatory results to other figures active in the first decades of the twentieth century such as Sibelius, Nielsen, Vaughan Williams and Bax. Even Bartók, about whom a considerable theoretical literature already exists concerning his use of symmetrical scale-forms, could be profitably approached from this perspective. Such theoretical explanations might begin to unpick a whole repertoire that has hitherto not been particularly well served analytically, a rich corpus of works that, while ever popular with audiences, has been customarily relegated to a historiographic limbo between late-Romantic chromaticism and full-fledged atonality.[16]

Scalar modulation also forms a connecting, intermediary stage in this present study's broad movement from the consideration of added-note harmony as vertical *Klang* to the horizontal succession of chords. The following, final analytical chapter examines the role of systematised progressions from one chord to another through interval cycles, above all the role of chromatic lines in Grieg's music. In effect, the focus on the diatonic scale-step of this preceding chapter is replaced by that on the chromatic step as underlying unit of measurement. It moreover returns to the important questions of line and register in Grieg's music, touched upon in the opening analysis of Op. 66 No. 1 and closely connected to the notions of sonority and colour explored in the first chapter.

typescript catalogued alongside Beyer's transcriptions for Op. 66, accessible online at http://brgbib.bergen.folkebibl.no/arkiv/grieg/notemanuskript/stor_66_tekster.pdf.

[16] Again, some of these points are elaborated upon in my study 'Monotonality and Scalar Modulation in Sibelius's *Tapiola*'.

3

Systematisation: Chromaticism, interval cycles and linear progressions

The Norwegian composer David Monrad Johansen introduces his 1934 biography of his most celebrated predecessor with an enigmatic reference to 'the greatest problem' modern music presents. Harmony has developed the purely colourful 'with startling rapidity' in the nineteenth century; however, the 'art of line' or counterpoint has remained stationary since Bach and Handel. The most pressing technical problem that composers have faced since the end of the Romantic era is hence how to create an 'art of line' that would not only control and structure but further incorporate and 'allow free play to all the countless shades of colour which the newly gained knowledge of the whole harmonic system has placed at our disposal'.[1] Strangely, Johansen neither explicitly connects Grieg to this issue nor goes on to explain what relevance it holds within the remaining four-hundred pages of his volume, but it is certainly curious and surely significant to read this on the first page of a book about Grieg.

For one of the greatest compositional problems present by the end of Grieg's life – recognised by theorists as diverse as Schoenberg, Schenker and Kurth, to equally diverse conclusions – was this problem of succession. As explained earlier, in an idiom in which the number of pitches accepted as consonant in vertical sonorities had greatly expanded, and the means for linking these chords grown ever more numerous as chromatic voice leading took over from functional root progressions, logical rationale for controlling the succession of chords and delimiting the apparent superabundance of harmonic possibility

[1] Johansen, *Edvard Grieg*, p. 3 (the first Norwegian edition dates from 1934, the English translation from four years later). Johansen is a problematic figure in many ways, given – for better or worse – his growing support for extreme right-wing politics in the late 1930s, and the potential ideological implications of his views on music history should not be ignored. Nevertheless, his account of Grieg still contains many insights and the passage above touches on compositional problems that were pertinent to many post-Romantic composers, regardless of their position within the political spectrum.

were increasingly felt as necessary, at least for any composer attempting to structure musical forms beyond the scale of the aphoristic miniature or without the framework provided by a text.

Grieg's own music was frequently prone to high levels of chromaticism. Yet at the same time, he often appears to have tried to control this chromaticism by structuring it though systematic frameworks. One of the most important of such means is found in his use of lines formed from a single interval class or proceeding by single scale-step, whereby a succession of harmonies may be connected into a logical series (a feature which provides an important means of syntactic consistency that may aid listener comprehension). The following account of linear harmonic succession works successively through such means of organisation by increasing interval size. It starts with an extensive consideration of chromatic and diatonic lines, moves more briefly through the third-shifts typifying the nineteenth century's second practice, and ends with Grieg's systematic exploitation of fifth movement and exploration of the limits of first-practice functionality.

Chromatic Lines

Chromaticism has long been seen as one of Grieg's distinctive traits, even though he is far from alone among his contemporaries in this respect. We recall Grieg's claim that 'a friend once told me I was "born chromatic"', and his early works, even those written before going to study in Leipzig, already reveal signs of this penchant.[2] Patrick Dinslage has pointed to the use of a falling chromatic bass line supporting seventh chords in the sixth of the *23 Short Pieces for Piano*, EG 104, 'Allegro con moto'.[3] Prophetic is also the last of this set, No. 23 'Assai allegro furioso' (1859), dating from the middle of Grieg's student years, in which the bass line is clearly constructed out of a descending $\hat{8}$–$\hat{5}$ ostinato line that soon becomes chromatically developed. Grieg relates how as a student he tried to make use of chromatic voice leading on every possible occasion in his chorale harmonisations, and the surviving exercises from Leipzig bear witness to this assertion.[4] While a general chromaticism typical of mid-nineteenth-century Romanticism may often be found pervading Grieg's early works (such as the celebrated song 'Jeg elsker dig', Op. 5 No. 3), what is most of interest here are the larger lines formed, especially descending ones in the bass, where one voice moves

[2] Letter to Finck, 17 July 1900, *Artikler og taler*, p. 52/*Letters to Colleagues and Friends*, p. 229.

[3] Patrick Dinslage 'Edvard Griegs Jugendwerk im Spiegel seiner Leipziger Studienjahre', *Svensk tidskrift för musikforskning*, 78 (1996), 36–7.

[4] Grieg, 'My First Success', *Artikler og taler*, p. 23/*Diaries, Articles, Speeches*, p. 81; see Dag Schjelderup-Ebbe, 'Neue Ansichten über die früheste Periode Edvard Griegs', *Dansk Aarbog for Musikforskning*, 1 (1961), 65–6 (the exercises are now housed in the Bergen Public Library). The most extended account of this early period is given by Schjelderup-Ebbe in *Edvard Grieg, 1858–1867*, which incorporates the material of the above article.

prominently through several degrees of the chromatic scale. Initially, one might suppose, the technique probably owes to a delight in the sheer sound of such slipping chromatic progression – in *Klang* – rather than consciously forming a way of connecting and thus ensuring the rational cohesion of successive harmonies. But later in Grieg's career this second implication gets taken up and developed in its own right.

In its simplest form, the chromatic descending bass often grows out of an $\hat{8}$–$\hat{5}$ descent used approaching a cadence, the chromatic alteration of degrees $\hat{7}$ and $\hat{6}$ being quite routine in the minor. In its own right, the progression has a long provenance from the Phrygian cadence leading *attacca* to the next section in the Baroque suite or da capo aria, and in Grieg's music it may either be followed by a brief functional fifth progression to strengthen the dominant or result directly in a perfect cadence. 'Jølstring' ('Wedding March from Jølster') from the *25 Norske Folkeviser og Danser,* Op. 17 No. 5, is a good example of the former paradigm, providing an early instance of the type of chromatic ostinato pattern that would become characteristic of Grieg (Ex. 3.1). Initially given in an ostinato inner voice doubled in thirds, from b. 9 the chromatic line from $\hat{7}$ to $\hat{5}$ is taken down into the bass, where, now essentially diatonic, it reaches $\hat{3}$ before leading to a clear cycle-of-fifths progression and perfect cadence to the tonic (I^6–VI–ii–V–i).

The linear descending bass followed by strong cadential fifth motion forms a powerful harmonic paradigm. Something similar was used in the final 'Allegro con moto' of the *23 Short Pieces for Piano,* and the same basic principles were even observed in the opening analysis of Op. 66 No. 1's 'Kulokk', where despite the much greater development of colouristic and linear elements the underlying structure (in this case diatonic) was in essence identical. Indeed, this paradigm can be found in both chromatic and diatonic forms throughout Grieg's oeuvre: the opening phrase of his first published piece, for instance – the *Klavierstück,* Op. 1 No. 1 – balances a distinctive linear descent (bb. 1–4) with a strong cycle of fifths progression to the imperfect cadence in b. 9. Generic precedent may be found in much nineteenth-century repertoire, perhaps most clearly the music of Chopin.[5]

Without a subsequent cycle of fifths, any chromatic element becomes intensified at the expense of the diatonic. A fine example from Grieg's later music is provided by the lugubrious closing descent of 'I Balladetone' ('In Ballad Style'), Op. 65 No. 5 (Ex. 3.2). At some stage in its development we might hypothesise that this paradigm gets transferred from a simple $\hat{8}$–$\hat{5}$ to a more radical $\hat{5}$–$\hat{1}$ or even $\hat{8}$–$\hat{1}$ chromatic

[5] The closing phrase of Chopin's C minor Prelude, Op. 28 No. 20, for instance, provides a relatively straightforward example of this model, while the late Mazurka in F minor, Op. 68 No. 4, intensifies the chromatic slipping (here of parallel seventh chords) in a manner far more typical of Grieg's practice. Jim Samson provides an apt summary of the F minor Mazurka from the perspective of its complementary relationship of chromatic and diatonic modes of behaviour in *Music in Transition: A Study of Tonal Expansion and Atonality, 1900–1920* (London: Dent, 1977), pp. 3–4.

Example 3.1 Grieg, 'Jølstring', *25 Norwegian Folksongs and Dances,* Op. 17 No. 5

Example 3.2 Grieg, 'In Ballad Style', *Lyric Pieces,* bk. VIII, Op. 65 No. 5, final cadence

descent. An intermediate stage may be witnessed in 'Erotikk', Op. 43 No. 5 (Ex. 3.3). Quite sumptuous is the effect in the closing two bars of chromatically slipping sevenths in the major, with a bass line that fills out the $\hat{5}$–$\hat{3}$ stage chromatically before implying the remaining $\hat{3}$–$\hat{1}$ through more traditional fifth root progression. What is typical of the earlier Grieg is that the succession of harmonies is not simply created by the parallel movement of block chords but is in fact highly functional in its implications.

The bass line fills out the $\hat{5}$–$\hat{1}$ space while simultaneously suggesting an almost complete cycle of fifths (taking into account chromatic alterations and melodic suspensions). The closing $\mathrm{iii}^{7\text{–}ø7}$–$\mathrm{VI}^{7}$–$\mathrm{ii}^{ø7}$–$\mathrm{V}_{4}$–$^{7}_{3}$–I progression is clearly apparent, if opulently adorned with half-diminished sonorities and suspensions, while the starting point, an F major $^{6}_{4}$ is unproblematic as an initial tonic. The two chords unaccounted for between these stages are more complex, though the second of these (b. 35, fourth semiquaver) is evidently a French sixth equivalent to an altered vii^7, thus extending the cycle of fifths back one further stage.[6] More unusual is the chromatic slipping of the $^6_4$ chord on the third semiquaver of b. 35, with the resulting parallel F$^6_4$–E$^6_4$ progression. It would be tempting to read the latter as some type of altered subdominant chord, thereby connecting the inverted I of the first harmony with the altered vii^7 of the third, resulting in an entire cycle of diatonically enclosed fifths. More immediately plausible would be to read this chord as an E–D suspension over an implied diminished seventh {F, G♯, B♮ [D]} supporting the melodic motion from $\hat{8}$ to $\hat{5}$, a pattern familiar in late Romantic music (one might recall Tristan's 'Ach, Isolde!' in Act III Scene 1 of Wagner's opera).[7] In Grieg's example, however, the suspended E is resolved onto a harmony that has already slipped chromatically onto the next chord in the cycle. Yet as the diminished seventh (only ever implicit here) is polysemous in root, we could easily read its B♮ as expressing a ♯IV function, thus completing the projected cycle of fifths after all, even while these bars bathe in their languorously chromatic idiom.

Example 3.3 Grieg, 'Erotic', *Lyric Pieces*, bk. III, Op. 43 No. 5, approach to final cadence

As the majority of the examples above imply, the usual syntactic position of such chromatic progressions is as an end gesture, forming the penultimate stage in a phrase where the tonally destabilising chromaticism may be brought under the control of a function progression. Both through their conventional association with cadential approaches, as likewise through their intrinsic properties (such as the strong subdominant tendencies of the flattened $\hat{7}$ and $\hat{6}$ degrees and the sense of repose resulting from the descending motion), the placement of such chromatic passages towards the end of phrases or pieces seems to make sense. So when such paradigms are encountered in an

[6] Sawyer, 'The Tendencies of Modern Harmony', 79, likewise comments 'The piano piece "Erotik" ... has the following termination, containing, among other points of interest, a 7th on the supertonic with flattened 5th'.

[7] The connotations of such an allusion, given the title of Grieg's piece, may not be coincidental.

opening passage we might ask to what end, to what expressive function, they are being used.

In the major, the association of this chromatic descending pattern with closure can easily create a nostalgic, retrospective quality. A perfect example is given by the opening to 'Solveig's Cradle Song' (*Solveigs Vuggesang*), the last number from Grieg's incidental music to Ibsen's *Peer Gynt* (Ex. 3.4), which opens with what sounds like a concluding phrase. The bass's $\hat{6}$–$\flat\hat{6}$–$\hat{5}$ descent, continued down to the tonic degree, creates a nostalgic glow intermixed with a curious touch of longing ideally suited to the song's closing function within the five-act play. At the song's close the chromaticism of this passage is further intensified. Even at a far smaller level, the opening $\hat{6}$–$\flat\hat{6}$–$\hat{5}$ descent alone may imbue the ensuing music with a wistful tone, as is epitomised in 'Våren' ('Spring'), Op. 33 No. 2, perhaps Grieg's most beloved song.

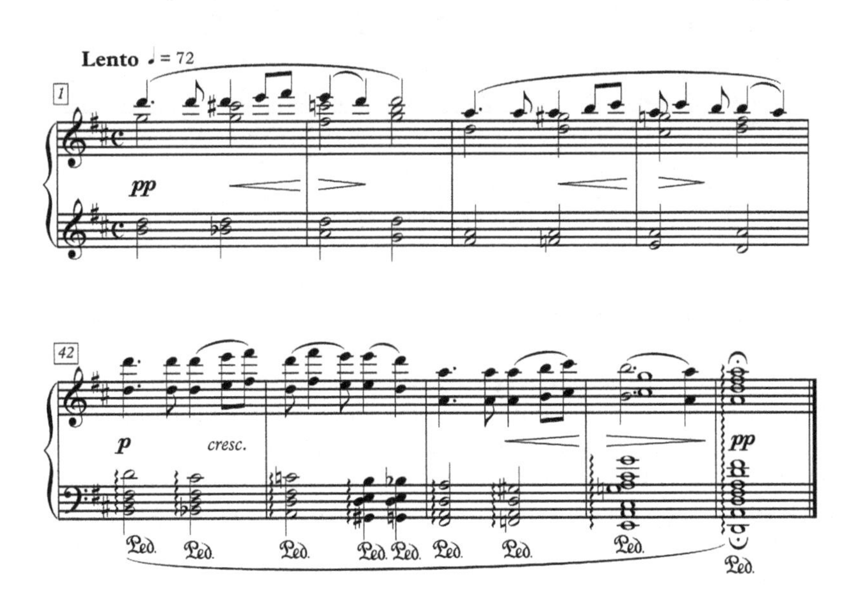

Example 3.4 Grieg, 'Solveig's Cradle Song', *Peer Gynt*, Op. 23 No. 23, opening and close

In the minor the effect can often be darker. A sense of pastness, loss or grief may be projected by a work that starts with this descending chromatic pattern (whose overlap with the $\hat{8}$–$\hat{5}$ descent of the *lamento* bass is plain). A melding of chromaticism with a diatonic descending line in the bass, comparable if freer to that glimpsed in Op. 17's 'Jølstring', may be seen in the opening number from the last book of *Lyric Pieces*, 'Der var engang' ('Once upon a Time'), Op. 71 No. 1, a piece from the end of Grieg's life. Here the bass line extends across almost an entire octave, descending from an e^1 $\hat{8}$ through seven intervening pitches to the Neapolitan f$\natural$, before a sequential 3–5 linear intervallic pattern leads to a strong perfect cadence in E minor (Ex. 3.5). Inverting this trajectory, the answering melodic phrase (bb. 4^1–8) makes as if to rise, yet ultimately this proves a vain endeavour. The past is closed off, slipping away, ever-dissipating before our eyes.

Example 3.5 Grieg, 'Once upon a Time', *Lyric Pieces*, bk. X, Op. 71 No. 1, opening

A similar effect to Op. 71 No. 1 is given earlier in the descending chromaticised bass line that underpins 'Den Bergtekne' ('The Mountain Thrall'), Op. 32, a piece that stands as one of Grieg's most concentrated and personal utterances. But perhaps the highpoint of Grieg's early use of descending chromatic lines is his harmonisation of the theme on which the Op. 24 *Ballade* is based (a folksong from Valders, taken from L.M. Lindeman's collection of Norwegian folk-tunes which had already provided the source for the Op. 17 settings). As with the paradigm in 'Solveig's Cradle Song', Grieg's bass starts by tracing a chromaticised $\hat{6}$–$\hat{1}$ descent, but here the line is continued further, opening up new harmonic depths (Ex. 3.6).

The original folk-melody clearly breaks into two matching four-bar phrases each of which end on the tonic, while the internal construction of these units is similarly repetitive, the second bar repeating the motivic cell of the first. Yet Grieg's harmonisation – mildly uncharacteristically – rides over the four-square nature of the given material through its intricate harmonic elision of the two phrases and the unusual metric complexity created by hemiola patterns in the harmonic rhythm. Across the opening phrase the harmonies arising from the descending bass line obfuscate the notated downbeats and triple metre by frequently suggesting paired groupings of crotchets, whose first chord resolves by step to its companion (a feature particularly prominent in bb. 2^3–4^3). Initially articulating two Phrygian $\flat\hat{6}$–$\hat{5}$ bass

Example 3.6 Grieg, *Ballade*, Op. 24, opening theme (first half)

progressions in G minor and F, the descending bass line continues through iv and V^4_2 to a first-inversion G minor, passes on through a whole-tone augmented-sixth substitute and an Italian sixth to a root-position G major, then resolves through a comparable French sixth to F major (b. 4^1), thus offering a parallel to the opening G–F sequence. The result of this constant uncertainty between triple and duple metre is that the melodic $\hat{2}$ on the downbeat of b. 4 is felt as a brief point of repose rather than an accented passing note to the final $\hat{1}$ on the second beat, the latter made to sound like ii^4_2 in an F major context. Two 'vagrant' half-diminished sevenths (bb. 4^3 and 5^1) blur the join to the reiteration of the phrase: the second of these easily becomes reinterpreted as an enriched ii^4_2–V in the return of the Phrygian progression that opened the theme. Apart from the new chromatic passing notes the repetition of the first two bars in bb. 5–6 is essentially identical. A simpler $\hat{8}$–♮$\hat{7}$–♮$\hat{6}$–♭$\hat{6}$–$\hat{5}$ descent, strengthened in octaves, underpins the ending.

In this manner Grieg skilfully avoids articulating the strongly implied tonic at the end of the first four-bar unit, and through his manipulation of harmonic rhythm and the linear unfolding of the bass creates the larger continuity of an eight-bar phrase that comes to a satisfactory close only in its final bar. This passage is a good paradigm of Grieg's earlier chromaticism in that the linear writing is not entirely systematic but still retains strong aspects of functionality, while his employment of augmented-sixth chords that resolve directly onto local tonics (rather than to the fifth degree) is typical of Romantic chromatic practice. The use of a simple melody as a thread on which a sinking, predominantly chromatic bass is hung points the way to many later examples of this technique in Grieg.

So far a number of analyses have shown how Grieg uses descending chromatic or chromaticised diatonic lines functionally within his music, especially in works dating from his first two creative decades. Such features are characteristic of Grieg, if hardly a radical departure from customary Romantic practice. But in Grieg's later music the chromatic line may easily become more systematically employed as an element in its own right, existing outside any functional tonal progression. Something of this contrast is already contained in the *Ballade,* in the passage of chromatically ascending V^7 chords found at bb. 210–14 (see Ex. 1.2). The non-functional, systematic nature of this brief passage forms a pointed parallelism with later examples of this type of procedure; Grieg's composition contains both the older, functional use of chromatic lines and emergent signs of more extreme techniques of intervallic succession taken beyond tonal function.

A prime example of such systematic use typical of the later Grieg may be found in the 'Kulokk' opening the second of the *Two Nordic Melodies,* Op. 63 (1895). The relatively simple melody, alternating conjunct motion around degrees $\hat{3}$ to $\hat{5}$ with the broken tonic triad, gives little hint of the increasingly chromatic treatment to which Grieg will subject it. Schjelderup-Ebbe finds this piece highly representative of Grieg's chromatic technique: 'one would not expect this diatonic, rather insignificant melodic line to possess possibilities for an interesting harmonic treatment … The use of a chromatic bass line is quite characteristic of Grieg'.[8] In fact so much of the meaning and expressive force of Grieg's setting is created through the syntactical implications of his harmonisation, whereby early touches of chromaticism develop into its wholesale manifestation by the end of the phrase.

The chromatic passage in question is that stretching from b. 19 to b. 22^1, outlining a near octave descent in the bass from F♮ to G (Ex. 3.7a). In contrast to virtually all Grieg's earlier examples, the line here is entirely chromatic, without a hint of a functional fifth progression or tonal pedal. Arguably more radical still, the associated harmonies are created as a rule through the block transfer of a seventh-chord sonority (minus the fifth) – a {0,4,10} cell – technically equivalent to an Italian sixth.[9] Only the triadic melody in the upper line (a typical cow-calling figure) provides any tonal thread to support the subsiding lower voices.

Ex. 3.7b shows the underlying paradigm utilised by Grieg in these bars. It is noteworthy, however, that despite the consistency of the bass's chromatic descent, in several places Grieg discreetly modifies the model by missing out a chromatic step in the inner voices, or by

[8] Schjelderup-Ebbe, *A Study of Grieg's Harmony*, p. 47.

[9] Similar passages of descending seventh-type chords may admittedly be encountered in earlier Romantic music – see for instance the chromatic sequence of German sixths and dominant sevenths in Chopin's A♭ major Prelude, bb. 24–6 – but there the chromatic alterations still serve highly functional ends. In Grieg the latter quality is largely shunned.

anticipating or retarding them through melodic suspensions. His deviations from the hypothetical model appear to be made in the interests of momentary tonal clarification. While the underlying principle behind this passage is unquestionably the non-functional, semitonal shifting of this seventh-chord sonority (rather than the complex, though nonetheless still functional, behaviour of harmonies combined around a flexible chromatic/diatonic line seen at the opening of the earlier *Ballade*), the paradigm is treated with sufficient flexibility for it to accommodate tonal implications throughout.

Example 3.7a Grieg, 'Kulokk', *Two Nordic Melodies*, Op. 63 No. 2/i

Example 3.7b Harmonic paradigm underpinning Grieg's 'Kulokk', Op. 63 No. 2/i, bb. 19–23

Thus, the opening harmony is built upon the flattened seventh degree – an apt choice for the subdominant tendencies of a concluding phrase; the middle of the passage passes reassuringly through a tonic second inversion (b. 20^5 – the metric strength of this arrival is hidden by the suspension on the preceding quaver beat); and the final, chromatically attained tonic is reached directly through a French sixth. Grieg's use of what is equivalent to and may thus multitask as either a seventh or as an (Italian) augmented sixth allows such tonal flexibility, especially when the potential additional pitch provided in the melody, or momentary modifications to the paradigmatic lines, are taken into account. But there has been a definite shift in governing principle from Op. 24 to Op. 63: a distinct chromatic line now affords functional behaviour, rather than a freer, partially chromatic line being sanctioned by a prevailing (albeit wandering) tonal functionality.

Of note here is also the sophisticated manner in which the harmonic rhythm of the chromatic seventh paradigm is manipulated by the composer in order to create first an acceleration and then a deceleration towards the end of the phrase. Such a pattern closely conforms to classical models for the harmonic rhythm of phrase units operating in a closing-cadential function. Reducing the superimposed rhythmic levels created by the interaction of the melody's variable rhythmic values and its internal suspensions and anticipations to the most basic template, we observe an underlying model akin to that given in Ex. 3.7c.

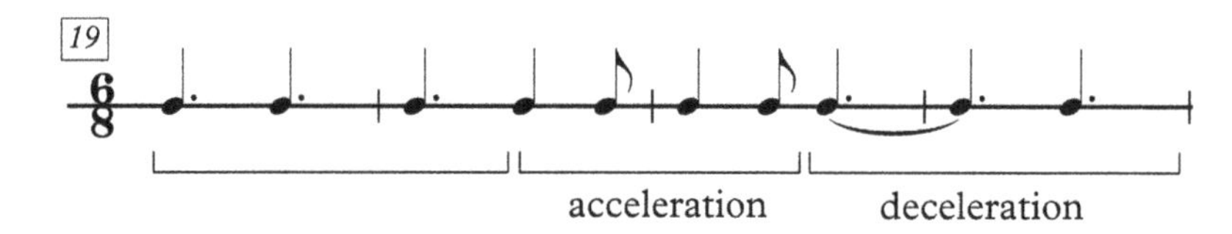

Example 3.7c Rhythmic paradigm underpinning Grieg's 'Kulokk', Op. 63 No. 2/i, bb. 19–22

A quickening of harmonic rhythm is observed across the second and third bars of the model, creating a hypermetric syncopation that ultimately aids the reduction in momentum towards the final cadence of the seventeen-bar melody. The *ben tenuto* designation over the bars of acceleration smoothes over the transition to the increased rate of harmonic movement; it is followed by an even more extreme (*molto*) retardation, elongating the final dotted crotchet (which thus approaches the preceding tied pair in duration). The descending chromatic progression, itself extendable indefinitely, is metrically articulated so as to come to a halt on the tonic. In an idiom in which functional behaviour is severely weakened, such extraneous, non-harmonic means of 'applying the brakes' become ever more useful for articulating formal boundaries.

Something of the nature of Grieg's later chromatic usage may be gleaned from comparing his Op. 63 setting of this tune with the far simpler harmonisation in Op. 17 (1869; Ex. 3.8). Again, the chromaticism of the final melodic phrase grows out of the smaller chromatic lines present near the end of the opening phrase units (bb. 5–6, 9–10^1), but the chromatic passage of bb. 15–18^1 is essentially one chromatic descending inner voice F♮–B doubled on two occasions in thirds, tonally supported over a V pedal and leading to a cadential fifth progression (bb. 17–18^1). While certainly chromatic, there is nothing in Op. 17 No. 22 of the systematic aspect characterising Op. 63 No. 2.

Even the very opening of Grieg's Op. 63 setting reveals the new intervallic systematisation at work in his later music. The four introductory bars split into three distinct intervallic layers fanning out from the initial b^1. A fifth cycle is formed in the bass, b^1–e–A–D–G^1 (initially created out of two thirds: the $e\flat^1$ in b. 2 humorously overshoots the expected diatonic third to $e\natural^1$, being immediately corrected an octave lower);[10] a chromatic line descends from the 'wrong' $e\flat^1$ of b. 2, $e\flat^1$–d^1–$c\sharp^1$–$c\natural^1$–b^1 (incompletely paralleled in the upper g^1–$f\sharp^1$ line); while the initial b^1 remains constant.

This separation out into constituent intervallic elements is yet more transparent in the ensuing 'Stabbelåten' ('Peasant Dance'), which forms the second part of Op. 63 No. 2 (Ex. 3.9). Rustic-sounding violin fifths give way to a repeated chromatic descent that rematerialises (inverted) in the ascending chromatic ostinato line of the melody's opening phrase (bb. 21ff), and (directly) as the descending ostinato of the refrain-like idea (bb. 28ff), which similarly fills out a tritone space chromatically. Again, nothing of this is prefigured in Grieg's earlier setting of the tune in Op. 17 No. 18, where the same rising chromatic ostinato is merely followed by mild chromatic neighbour-note shimmying at the end of the refrain. In short, Op. 63 displays far more compositional intervention than the 1871 settings in its systematic exploration of intervals *qua* independent elements and not merely tonal constituents, a technique that points forward to the Op. 72 *Slåtter.*

'Notturno', from the fifth book of *Lyric Pieces*, Op. 54 No. 4, shows an elaboration of the chromatic descending seventh paradigm witnessed

[10] Continuing the fifth cycle, the next subsequent pitch in the bass is indeed c in b. 9.

Example 3.8 Grieg, 'Kulokk', *25 Norwegian Folksongs and Dances*, Op. 17 No. 22

in Op. 63's 'Kulokk'. In bb. 48–54 an entire octave g–G is chromatically composed out in the bass through this descending seventh pattern, now melodically decorated with 'Chopin' $\hat{3}$–$\hat{2}$ suspensions over every alternate V^7 chord (Ex. 3.10b).

This chromatic purple passage is here even more evidently the result of a compositional process operating across the piece, whereby a chromatic scalic descent from $\hat{8}$ to $\hat{5}$ that underpins the opening two-bar melodic unit is gradually extended (a process similar to that seen in Op. 66 No. 14, if more straightforward here). Following the repetition in bb. 3–4 of the opening figure – now decorated melodically with

Example 3.9 Grieg, 'Stabbelåten', *Two Nordic Melodies,* Op. 63 No. 2/ii

Example 3.10a Grieg, 'Notturno', *Lyric Pieces*, bk. V, Op. 54 No. 4, bb. 1–14

the 'Grieg Leitmotiv'[11] – the chromatic descent it initiated continues in a tenor line from the g reached in b. 4 (f♯–f♮–e–e♭–d, bb. 5–9), while the bass commences another descent from c in stretto with the tenor line (Ex. 3.10a). The latter's final stage, the resolution onto the newly tonicised G, is delayed until the end of the section (b. 14), where the

Example 3.10b Grieg, 'Notturno', *Lyric Pieces*, bk. V, Op. 54 No. 4, bb. 46–63

[11] The 'Grieg Leitmotiv' (so styled after Monrad Johansen) refers to a descending $\hat{8}$–$\hat{7}$–$\hat{5}$ figure, typically A–G♯–E as in the opening to the Piano Concerto (and as found here in 'Notturno'). See also Jing-Mao Yang, *Das 'Grieg Motiv' – Zur Erkenntnis von Personalstil und musikalischem Denken Edvard Griegs* (Kassel: G. Bosse, 1998), pp. 1–4 (who strangely does not mention Johansen).

Example 3.10b (*Continued*)

coincidence of the tenor d and bass G is nicely smudged by the reiteration of the tenor's last chromatic step e♭–d.

The climactic passage in question comes at the end of the reprise of this A section and leads into a coda (bb. 55ff) that gently reconfigures the opening chromatic $\hat{8}$–$\hat{5}$ paradigm alongside the colouristic common-tone shifts and mediant relations that had characterised the central B section. The F^7 (or twin root F+a) in b. 56 introduces a subdominant-side relaxation intermixed with the submediant that since the opening has been blurred within the tonic realm, while the common-tone-related A♭ superimposition on the F–C dyad (b. 59) might refer back to the flat submediant (A♭^{9}) of bb. 25–6. Finally the modified C–e^6_3 –C cadence at the end balances the pronounced mediant harmony of the B section ($E^{9/11}$, bb. 21–4) and gently undercuts any dominant strength with the more amorphous mediant.

Grieg's most extreme use of this chromatically shifting seventh paradigm, however, in both ascending and descending form, is encountered in the closing eight bars of his setting of 'Siri Dale Visen' ('The Song of Siri Dale'), Op. 66 No. 4. Asbjørn Eriksen describes this passage as 'probably the most striking and most frequently discussed example of this kind of harmony in Grieg'.[12] One might go further to call them the most discussed bars of Griegian harmony in scholarship *tout court*. Ernst Kurth, Kurt von Fischer, Dag Schjelderup-Ebbe, Carl Dahlhaus, Jørgen Jersild, Ekkehard Kreft, Jing-Mao Yang, Daniel Grimley, Kevin

[12] Asbjørn Ø. Eriksen, 'Griegian Fingerprints in the Music of Frederick Delius (1862–1934)', paper presented at the International Grieg Society Conference, Bergen 30 May 2007, www.griegsociety.org/default.asp?kat=1009&id=4515&sp=2, p. 8.

Swinden and Eriksen himself have all grappled with the recalcitrant chromaticism of these bars.

Nowhere does Grieg's claim to have found the hidden harmonies in Norwegian folk music appear more strained – or at least inadequate as a primary explanation – when we compare the simple, sixteen-bar melody he took as his starting point with the harmonic result of his compositional daring (Ex. 3.11a and 3.11b). Beyer's version suggests a very mild ambivalence over the $\hat{6}$ and $\hat{7}$ degrees in the minor (hardly unusual),[13] but aside from the chromatic sharpening of $\hat{4}$ when leading up to $\hat{5}$ there is little here that would imply the extreme chromaticism that overtakes the end of Grieg's arrangement. Grimley has pointed to the text of the song (which speaks of the protagonist's sad love aged seventeen and souring of his life ever since) as a possible cause, and certainly the expressive trajectory of the text, allied with Grieg's propensity for chromatic streams of sevenths, explains the choice of harmonisation as well as any mystical encounter with the harmonic essence of Norwegian peasantry or landscape.[14]

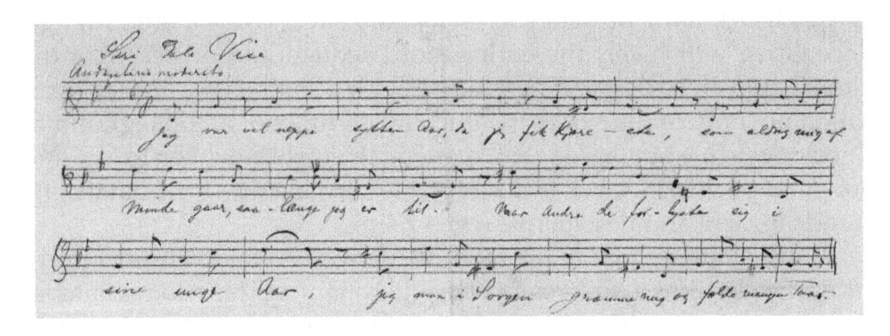

Example 3.11a 'Siri Dale Visen', original transcription by Frants Beyer

Most remarkable here is the sheer uncompromising nature of the chromatic operations on the {0,4,10} chord in bb. 15–22, which is ramped up by step through a tritone from G to d♭ and symmetrically down again. Kreft rightly points out that this single-minded pursuit of harmonic succession was not present in early Grieg.[15] If the chromatic paradigm witnessed in Op. 63's 'Kulokk' and Op. 54's 'Notturno' still retained some functional interpretation of the individual harmonic entities arising from the linear progressions, 'Siri Dale Visen' makes no such conces-

[13] Grieg ignores what appears to be a natural sign before the f^1 in b. 3 of the melody, though this may well be a poorly written sharp (a natural would not need to be given here).

[14] Grimley, *Grieg: Music, Landscape and Norwegian Identity*, pp. 101–2. As mentioned above, transcriptions of all the texts accompanying the original songs used in Op. 66 may be found in the Bergen Public Library (http://brgbib.bergen.folkebibl.no/arkiv/grieg/notemanuskript/stor_66_tekster.pdf).

[15] Kreft, *Griegs Harmonik*, p. 220. The one possible exception is 'Klokkeklang', Op. 54 No. 6, analysed later.

sion to functional etiquette. As Grimley has demonstrated, the passage could easily be rewritten to accommodate tonal function by modifying the strict intervallic logic applied to the basic pattern, but this is not what Grieg does.[16] It is arguable that several chords in this sequence are in fact 'atonal', in that they arise merely from the abstract intervallic law set up by the composer rather than bearing any conceivable functional relation to either melody or their neighbouring harmonies.

Several instances of the Italian sixth or incomplete dominant-seventh chord in these bars could be functional, but they are rarely connected functionally. Grieg's opening I7♮is in itself hardly outlandish: as we have seen, a subdominant-tending chord is a plausible initial harmony for this chromatic seventh paradigm. Moving out to an Italian sixth is more surprising, though in voice-leading terms again reasonable. The only curiosity here is the order of the two chords. In fact, as the next harmony in the sequence is functionally a pre-dominant on II, the opening three chords make perfect sense in retrograde: a II^7 leads to an Italian sixth that functions as a tritone substitution for the dominant (the tritone {C, F♯} retained while the V D is replaced by a ♭II A♭). Heard in the present succession, the effect is just a little strange. Since Grieg will invert the entire chord sequence upon reaching the tritonal apex in b. 17, we are presented with a compelling musical realisation not only of the extent to which much functional tonal grammar is non-reversible but moreover the unequal weighting given to 'up' and 'down' in pitch terms. What is acceptable slipping down chromatically sounds bizarre and destructive when rising.

It is the fourth chord in the sequence, however, that really announces the departure into a new realm. This dissonant aggregation of pitches {B♭, A♭, D, F♯} arises purely out of the linear process set up: it simply makes no aural sense either individually as a chromatically altered $\mathrm{B}\flat^7$ harmony, or in terms of tonal succession as a $\mathrm{III}\sharp^{7}_{\sharp 5}$ connecting $\mathrm{II}^{9/7}$ and $\natural\mathrm{III}^{7}_{6}$. This ensuing $\mathrm{B}^{7}_{6[-5\ \mathrm{susp.}]}$ does at least sound consonant in its own right, but has no logical connexion with the entirely functional IV^7 that follows. Significantly, the harmonic rhythm set up, where two changes of harmony per bar lead to two per half bar at the start of b. 17, would easily accommodate a II^{6}_{5}–V–I cadence into the start of b. 18 [♩. ♪ | ♩ .], as would the melody's $\hat{2}$–$\hat{7}$–$\hat{1}$. Yet by pausing on the tritonally distant D♭ for two dotted crotchets before descending the way it came, the progression refrains from composing out any deeper tonal linear progression. The only functional amelioration in the sequence is provided in its final bar (b. 20), where the voice leading is modified to aid the preparation of the concluding plagal cadence (the tenor's expected F♯ given in the melodic line on the final beat of the bar).

While some analysts (especially those in the post-Riemann tradition) attempt to find functional grounds for every chord here, even if every pitch might be altered from its hypothetical basis, this surely

[16] Grimley, *Grieg: Music, Landscape and Norwegian Identity*, p. 100.

Example 3.11b Grieg, 'Siri Dale Visen', *19 Norwegian Folksongs,* Op. 66 No. 4

misses the point.[17] At some stage, to reuse a Schoenbergian mythic archetype, the Procrustean bed of tonal function simply becomes too strained. By the fourth chord in Grieg's progression, the logic of

[17] See Jørgen Jersild, *De funktionelle principper i romantikkens harmonik: belyst med udgangspunkt i César Franck's harmoniske stil* (Copenhagen: Wilhelm Hansen, 1970), p. 56 (though Jersild's pointing to the use of tritone substitution in interpreting these chords is perceptive); Yang, *Das 'Grieg Motiv'*, pp. 158–61. Kevin J. Swinden both problematises and offers functional and Schenkerian readings of the passage in 'Toward Analytic Reconciliation of Outer Form, Harmonic Prolongation and Function', *College Music Symposium,* 45 (2005), 108–23.

'n+1' (where n is a {0,4,10} chord and 1 designates a step on the series of twelve chromatic pitches) indubitably takes over. Ernst Kurth's description of one of the primary causes in the Romantic dissolution of functional tonality is fitting here: the 'lines often assume primary importance for entire passages, and produce the harmonic progression as a by-product'.[18]

Kurth actually devotes a short analysis to this piece in *Romantische Harmonik* as an illustration of 'how tonal relations ebb away within linear currents and loose their centricity'.[19] Kurth appears relatively positive in attempting a functional definition of Grieg's chords, but his wider argument points to this type of sequence as leading to the undermining of tonality. For his younger colleague Kurt von Fischer, however, an underlying functional interpretation of these bars becomes more problematised. Though the melody functions as a 'type of cantus firmus over the splintering of tonal relations', Fischer also notes that it often proceeds 'without any regard for the underlying chords', 'in whose course no tonal stopping point may be detected'.[20]

The evident dichotomy here is left unexplored by Fischer, but this feature of Grieg's harmonic style was taken up by Carl Dahlhaus, whose notable analysis of this passage is worth quoting at length. If anything, Dahlhaus reads Grieg's practice here as historically more drastic than Kurth had believed. Already in the fourth of Grieg's *Norske Fjeldmelodier*, 'Sigurd and the Troll Bride' (EG 108a), Dahlhaus contends that

> harmony functions less as a foundation for the melody than vice-versa. The simplicity of the upper voice serves as a foothold without which the harmonic progression ... would remain dangling in mid-air. In this case, however, harmonic sophistication, brought about by tonally integrable dissonances, comes close to splitting the piece into unrelated 'layers', creating a bitonal dichotomy between late-romantic chromaticism and modal folk melody.

This 'rift between melody and harmony, a musical fait accompli in the aforementioned passage ... is part of an ongoing process in the fourth of Grieg's *Norwegian Folk Tunes*, Op. 66'.

> If the opening measure and a half still permits a functional interpretation (with G–D–A as a root progression), the parallel chords in the accompaniment gradually form a structural element in their own right as the simple G-minor harmony increasingly comes into conflict with the chromatic harmony.

Grieg's notation is therefore 'a façade behind which can be seen a harmonic mechanism bursting the bonds of tonality. Melodic pitches so straightforward as to have ineradicable tonal implications are forced into almost bizarre nonfunctional roles in the harmony'. Techniques

[18] Kurth, *Romantische Harmonik*, p. 353. Gregory Proctor makes a similar observation on Grieg's chromatic practice in regard to 'Gjætergut', Op. 54 No. 1 ('Technical Bases of Nineteenth-Century Chromatic Tonality', pp. 201–4).

[19] Kurth, *Romantische Harmonik*, p. 332 ('wie die tonalen Klangverhältnisse unter den lineare Strömungen verfließen und ihre Kernfestigkeit verlieren').

[20] Fischer, *Griegs Harmonik*, pp. 88, 87, 87.

'such as bitonality and chord streams' to which this gives rise anticipate the music of the twentieth century.[21]

Before this, Liszt was probably the only composer to conceive similarly abstract, intervallic constructive principles and apply them so uncompromisingly, in late piano works such as *Nuages Gris*. But what is distinctive in Grieg is that the more-or-less atonal is directly juxtaposed with the seemingly archaic and pre-tonal. As Dahlhaus's account indicates, this practice holds notable implications for the historical situation of Grieg's music and its own 'inner historicity' of material. From a progressive interpretation of music history the atavism embodied in Grieg's choice of melodic material looks curious alongside the extreme modernity of its treatment (to this extent something he has in common with Bartók and Stravinsky). Yet – as will be returned to in this study's conclusion – from a less judgemental perspective than that of a familiar modernist ideology Grieg can be seen as enriching the possibilities of how the polyvalent notion of tonality may be conceived. One might also see this curious admixture of the radically new and archaically backward in the music of Grieg's final years as exemplifying a characteristic trait of 'late style' – its untimeliness.

While dreaming up the Op. 66 settings during the Jotunheimen mountain trip in the summer of 1896, Grieg was also at work on an essay on Mozart.[22] 'With the exception of Bach,' Grieg claims here, 'no one has understood how to use the chromatic scale as well as Mozart in order to express the highest in music.'[23] Grieg's self-professed fascination with chromatic lines in Op. 66 is indeed demonstrated in this set's use of this technique as their predominant constructive principle.[24] Virtually all the pieces in this collection possess a significant descending chromatic or diatonic line as one of their primary attributes.[25] The sheer ubiquity of this technique suggests that it might contain an important clue as to the grammatical structure of Grieg's later harmonic idiom, as well as the 'highest' effect he seems to have been driving at.

Approaching this question from the reverse perspective, in order to ascertain what this linear bass does – what it contributes to the music – we could ask what happens when it is missing. As noted, almost every

[21] Carl Dahlhaus, *Nineteenth-Century Music*, trans. J.B. Robinson (Berkeley and Los Angeles: University of California Press, 1989), pp. 309–10 (wording very slightly amended).

[22] Röntgen, *Grieg*, p. 56.

[23] Grieg, 'Wolfgang Amadeus Mozart' (1897): 'Med undtagelse af Bach ... har ingen forstået så godt som Mozart at anvende den kromatiske skala for at udtrykke det høieste i musik'; *Artikler og taler*, p. 157/*Diaries, Articles, Speeches*, p. 235.

[24] Grieg, letter to Finck, 17 July 1900, *Artikler og taler*, p. 52/*Letters to Colleagues and Friends*, p. 229.

[25] Several scholars have offered schematic overviews of Grieg's practice in this regard: see Peer Findeisen, 'Ethnofolkloristische Anmerkungen zu Griegs Klavierzyklus *19 norske folkeviser* op. 66', in Ekkehard Kreft (ed.), *Bericht des 1. Deutschen Edvard-Grieg-Kongresses* (Altenmedingen: Hildegard-Junker-Verlag, 1996), pp. 135–51, Kreft, *Griegs Harmonik*, pp. 218–21.

number in Op. 66 seems to feature this principle: even the harmonic richness of No. 18, 'Jeg går i tusind tanker', conceals a larger two-octave diatonic descent across its course. No. 7, 'Bådnlåt' ('Lullaby'), and No. 11, 'Der stander to Piger' ('There Stood Two Girls'), are two of the few exceptions, in that here the linear scalic element is relatively slight. The former, a simple, two-fold statement of a nine-bar melody in D minor, is given first in bare octaves and then harmonised in a simple manner, emphasising the overriding diatonicism by the use of an inner dominant pedal in the opening four bars. There is simply little space, or need, for introducing chromatic complications here. Although understated linear writing appears in passing in the middle of No. 11 (bb. 9–10), it certainly does not form a significant constructive principle in Grieg's setting, while unlike No. 7 the inner parts frequently move chromatically and the tonal stability offered by a pedal is absent. This might explain why the audible impression of this second piece is of a more wandering, nebulous tonality than is perhaps warranted by looking on the page. It is arguable whether 'Der stander to Piger' is in fact any more chromatic than several other pieces in the collection: it is just that the marked linear basis that could aid aural comprehension is missing. This interpretation seems to be borne out by comparing it with the fifth setting in the collection, 'Det war i min Ungdom' ('It was in my Youth'), in which a highly chromatic idiom, deriving in part from the non-diatonic folk material used (including a saturation of augmented seconds from the use of $\sharp\hat{4}$ in the minor), is nevertheless held together by the large-scale descending chromatic lines working in tandem between bass and tenor.

All these examples point to the idea that strongly profiled bass lines, even when highly chromatic and supporting parallel chord progressions, contribute a sense of logical order to the musical unfolding, while a comparable level of chromaticism, when not directed into larger lines, becomes disorientating. This may also help explain why this linear progression is normally found in the bass voice, since here it may contribute most powerfully to a sense of directional purposiveness underpinning the music. A revealing example of one of the few exceptions to this practice is found in Grieg's penultimate *Lyric Piece*, Op. 71 No. 6, 'Forbi' ('Gone'), which opens with a chromatic upper part moving in major thirds by semitonal step (Ex. 3.12).

Example 3.12 Grieg, 'Gone', *Lyric Pieces*, bk. X, Op. 71 No. 6, opening

Despite the initial 'atonal' progression giving way to elements of the cycle of fifths implied through the bass motion, and the linear composing out by chromatic step of the E minor tonic's fifth space b^1–e^1 in the melody, the effect of the chromaticism still seems less focused – aptly one might say, given the regretful tone of the piece, its sense of continual, inexorable slipping away.[26]

A further pertinent question is why the chromatic sequence almost always appears descending rather than rising. As 'Siri Dale Visen' shows, the ascending form sounds somehow far more dissonant, even aggressive in its tonally destructive intent, than the descending. One might appeal to a sense of 'tonal gravity': falling motion, presumably through cultural use and expectations, seems to lead more clearly to a state of rest. After all, orthodox Schenkerian theory exhibits descending *Urlinien*, not ascending ones. Similarly, in the passage cited earlier from Kurth, the theorist speaks of how 'everything streams *downwards*'; potential energy contained in chords is released in the kinesis of linear melodic movement, before a lower equilibrium is attained.[27] Adopting an overriding historical narrative, it would seem irresistible to connect this 'downward', entropic movement to the idea of the dissolution of tonality. The metaphorical nature of such language (the notions of 'up' and 'down' in pitch terms being themselves metaphorical) should not detract from its near-universal assumption and hence significance for our conceptualisation of music. More technically, however, the common tetrachordal composition of such harmonies might imply a remnant of functional behaviour still persisting from the rule that the seventh falls by step. Earlier instances of prolonged sequences of chromatically descending tetrachords (perhaps most prominently Chopin's E minor Prelude) revolve around the downward resolution of sevenths and other pitches treated as linear suspensions.[28] Even in augmented-sixth chords, where one voice may rise by chromatic step, one or more of the other voices descend, normally resulting in a net descent in pitches.

Paradoxical though it might seem, often such chromatic lines in Grieg appear to be used as a means to control chromaticism, or the apparently excessive amorphousness that could easily result from its overuse (and often did in post-Wagnerian music). The aural coherence provided by a regular – and thus predictable – succession of pitches in one line therefore compensates for the departure from functional practice; as Patrick McCreless sums it up, 'a unidirectional chromatic line in the melodic or bass voice can hold together a passage that is harmonically adventurous'.[29] It should come as no surprise that strongly linear chromatic writing, particularly in a bass voice, has a long provenance

[26] Noted also by Kreft, *Griegs Harmonik*, p. 224.

[27] Kurth, *Romantische Harmonik*, p. 353, my emphasis.

[28] On this point see again Tymoczko, *A Geometry of Music*, pp. 284–302.

[29] Patrick McCreless, 'Elgar and Theories of Chromaticism', in Julian Rushton and J.P.E. Harper-Scott (eds.), *Elgar Studies* (Cambridge: Cambridge University Press, 2007),

in the more loosely knit textures of fantasias or sonata development sections. As Kreft sees it (returning once more to the issues raised by Johansen), the use of colouristic harmony in Romantic music and associated love of surprise and unpredictability spills out of the use of these features in classical development sections, just as does the corresponding unifying principle of the chromatic linear bass.[30]

The fundamental point here is, in short, that the Romantic desire to connect vertical sonorities through chromatic (i.e. minimal) voice leading still does not adequately define for a composer what these harmonies could be. The refinements of recent Neo-Riemannian theories suggest ways of maintaining triadic writing within a chromatic idiom, but such principles are still quite broad in remit and do not restrict the range of choice that much. Given the multiple ways in which a triad or tetrachord may move smoothly to another, why does a composer choose one particular chord and not another? Not only by using a melody (such as a pre-existent folksong) as guiding thread or 'cantus firmus', but further by systematising chromatic lines, Grieg offers a practical solution.

Yet in itself, a chromatic logic of succession need not imply, let alone strengthen, a sense of tonality. Though the conjunct motion of voices and harmonic consistency found in Grieg's chromatic seventh paradigm form two of Tymoczko's components of tonality, they would make less of an impression without a third important element Grieg employs: pitch centricity.[31] Grieg wields his chromatic lines with a strong sense of directionality, their use aimed at the attainment of important structural pitches. Sutcliffe explains:

> Rather than using chromaticism for the purposes of momentary inflection or expansion of the harmonic sense ... the composer tends to proceed in a directed and directional way. Most commonly the chromaticism is used to intensify a linear progression in the bass, normally of an octave or fifth ... Thus the chromaticism is contained and made to serve functional rather than hedonistic ends, so to speak.[32]

Hence, Grieg's later chromatic practice retains conjunct movement and harmonic consistency in furtherance of tonal centricity, even if he often downplays harmonic consonance and macroharmonic economy in these passages. Noteworthy, too, is how often there is a non-chromatic limiting factor such as a pedal or a clearly demarcated

p. 5. McCreless points to the theoretical formulations of this trait by Schenker and Kurth (cf. pp. 18–19).

[30] Kreft, *Griegs Harmonik*, pp. 159ff.

[31] One should also note that the {0,4,10} collection is in itself relatively harmonically consonant, dividing the octave nearly evenly, thus fulfilling another of Tymoczko's categories. It is when this sonority is combined with pitches in the melody that the result may fluctuate between consonant and more dissonant states.

[32] Sutcliffe, 'Grieg's Fifth', 167–8. Kreft, too, has noted how Grieg's chromatic lines are characteristically goal-directed (*Griegs Harmonik*, p. 214).

registral space supporting tonal articulation.[33] In the composer's lifetime Sawyer had already commented on Grieg's 'favourite plan of making one or even two notes a kind of upper pedal, and letting the other parts progress chromatically up or down'.[34] As will be discussed presently, the *Slåtter* in particular make much use of such pedal points as a means of consolidating the music's tonal properties. Thus alongside the thread provided by a diatonic melody, goal-directed chromatic lines, pedals, and registral boundary play all create a firm tonal mooring and a drive towards hierarchical pitch centricity.

By way of illustrating this last point, a final example in this section, taken from one of Grieg's earlier piano pieces, will demonstrate how even early on in his career extensive chromatic writing may be extended into larger lines that are directed towards the attainment of tonally significant pitches. The F major *Album Leaf*, Op. 28 No. 2 (Ex. 3.13), forms an intensified version of the directed chromatic lines contained within Op. 5's 'Jeg elsker dig', and foreshadows the later *Lyric Piece* 'Secret' (Op. 57 No. 4).[35] While the lower appoggiaturas and rising chromatic lines of Grieg's piece clearly seem to take their bearings from *Tristan*, both the characteristic half-diminished seventh and the floating tonal idiom of the latter are conspicuously absent. In their place we find the liberal use of augmented triads and French-sixth sonorities, reflecting both the underlying major key and the chromatic decoration of essentially diatonic lines. What is nevertheless retained from Wagner's example is the lack of tonal confirmation: despite the clear sense of F major throughout, the home tonic is only sounded twice in passing as a second inversion (bb. 2^2 and 39^2) before the piece's final chord. This *Album Leaf* is nominally in F, but spends much of its course moving between V/F and C.

The opening melodic line is directed from an initial e^1 to an eventual goal of c^4 at b. 8. While the opening is largely chromatic, diatonicism soon asserts itself as an equally important principle. Stretches of the line traversed diatonically will often have the absent intervening chromatic steps filled in subsequently, however. For instance, the 'missing' $g\sharp^1$ in the opening bar is the one chromatic note provided by the tenor line ($a\flat^1$, b. 2), while the diatonic c^2–e^2 segment in b. 2 is the one stage of the ascent returned to, being chromatically filled in the following bar ($c\sharp^2$–d^2–$d\sharp^2$, b. 3). The first four bars in their entirety may be thought of as a registral expansion from e^1 to e^2 (with the pitch G

[33] The fact that the chromatic progression closing Op. 66 No. 4 ascends through the interval of a tritone before returning again underlines the non-functional, even gratuitous nature of its appearance, and correspondingly its exceptional quality within Grieg's practice.

[34] Sawyer, 'The Tendencies of Modern Harmony', 85.

[35] The connexion with the theme of *eros* is underscored by the existence of another version of this piece from the same year (1874) as a song, 'Den blonde Pige' ('The Blonde Girl'), EG 138, whose text by Bjørnson begins with the line 'Jeg elsker dig'.

forming a type of cover note over each), under which the opening C[7] harmony becomes more firmly established as C in its own right. The four-bar consequent (bb. 4[3]–8) develops the model by ornamenting the familiar rising line with contrary motion in the right hand, before taking up the line on f♯[3] an octave higher and soaring up further to the newly tonicised c[4] goal. The chromatic ascent, counterpoised with descending chromatic lines in inner parts, provides liberal opportunities for passing dissonances formed of double suspensions in the manner of *Tristan*, yet the clear tonal goal of the larger line imparts an overriding harmonic security.

Example 3.13 Grieg, *Four Album Leaves*, Op. 28 No. 2

Example 3.13 *(Continued)*

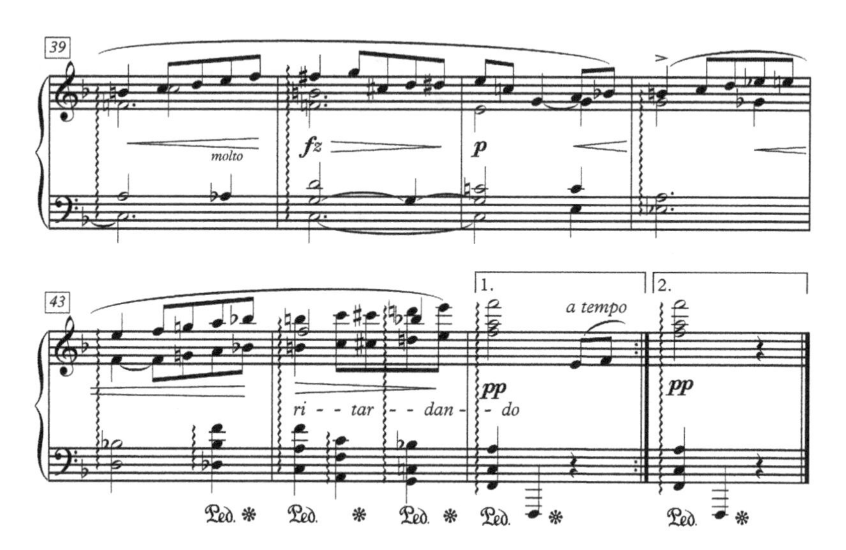

Example 3.13 (*Continued*)

The *Albumblad*'s central section is typical in its sequential construction and stacking up of supra-triadic entities (including a prominent V^{13}/V in b. 30 formed overtly of melodic thirds) before a functional discharge of this accumulated tension and return to the opening material. This climactic point in the retransition is noteworthy as the only instance in the entire piece of a half-diminished seventh (b. 35). Yet despite the implicit reference to *Tristan*, an unmistakably 'Norwegian' *kulokk* figure on top completely undercuts any suggestion of Wagnerian ethos clinging to the music. In general this *Albumblad* evinces a more urbane, controlled chromaticism for the salon (a feature highlighted by Grieg's elastic suppleness of rubato in a marvellous piano roll of him playing this piece), one yet carefully directed through the composer's mastery of large-scale linear writing.

Diatonic Lines and/or Larger Linear Sequences

While the overriding impression of Op. 66 is of a pronounced chromaticism in the descending bass lines, several of these are in fact diatonic, while others chromatically decorate an underlying diatonic basis (as in the example just given of Op. 28 No. 2). As raised earlier in the discussion of scalar modulation given in Chapter 2, both chromatic and diatonic lines may be conceived of as two different but relatable types of scalar collection. In one (diatonic), the measure of the scale-step is variable in intervallic content, normally ranging between semitone and tone and which thus may be more readily accommodated into a hierarchical system such as tonality; in the other (chromatic), a more abstract, systematic, and potentially 'atonal' procedure of succession prevails. Both forms of scalar organisation may be utilised by the composer to demarcate a larger registral space, just as seen in the second of the *Album Leaves*. In fact throughout his music Grieg is adept in using the two as complementary systems (comparable in this sense to Richard Cohn's understanding of late-Romantic bilinguality).[36]

This reciprocal relation between chromatic and diatonic lines is well illustrated in the modal A minor 'Melody' from the fourth book of *Lyric Pieces*, Op. 47 No. 3 (1888; Ex. 3.14). The two opening phrases (bb. 1–16) are supported by the diatonic descent from A through the equivalent of an octave in the bass line (only slightly obscured by the octave transferral from D to d in b. 9), this being split into two halves that articulate a i–V; iv–V/iv progression. In contrast, the answering phrase from b. 17 is formed from the slow ascent of the bass, now chromatically filling out the previously diatonic octave space under more expressive harmonies often of a half-diminished cast. This ascent is achieved by the use of a four-bar model treated in sequence up a minor third. Characteristic of the composer's practice, however, is that after three stages the pattern breaks down, Grieg avoiding a full octave division through the minor-third interval cycle. Thus, from b. 25 the bass progression becomes stalled on the f♭/e♮ degree $\hat{5}$, only at length breaking loose to an f♮ in b. 33. This pitch in fact forms the apex of the line, the bass line subsequently falling back towards the lower A, now by decreasing interval size f–d–c–B–B♭–A (minor third, tone, diatonic semitone, 'chromatic' semitone, 'chromatic' semitone). At the very end of this highly reiterative piece (bb. 95ff) this structurally salient F is repeatedly returned to in an uneasy Phrygian-coloured close.

Example 3.14 Grieg, 'Melody', *Lyric Pieces*, bk. IV, Op. 47 No. 3, opening

[36] Cohn, *Audacious Euphony*, pp. 199–210.

Example 3.14 (*Continued*)

As argued, despite appearing less systematic than chromaticism in its rationalisation of the unit of scalar distance, diatonic writing is just as powerful a means of linear articulation and may blend more smoothly with the *Klang* component of Grieg's harmonic style, creating acoustically consonant extended harmonies and, especially, macroharmonies (the tonal feature notably lacking in Grieg's chromatic seventh paradigm). Perhaps the fullest realisation of such diatonicism is to be encountered in the 'Gangar' from the fifth book of *Lyric Pieces*, Op. 54 No. 2 (Ex. 3.15).

Diatonic lines and interval cycles run throughout this piece, the wash of C major being relieved only momentarily by f♯[1] grace notes (aiding a passing tonicisation of the dominant at bb. 6–8), the colourful chromatic third shifts at bb. 17–25 (themselves forming an interval cycle), and the flat-submediant 'chromatic swerve' in bb. 68–72.[37] The opening succession of added-note sonorities created through the interplay of two lines in parallel sixths, pedal and diatonic melody, is a trait familiar from earlier accounts of Op. 66 Nos 1 and 14. Diatonic seventh chords on IV, ii and I are heard in the opening four bars, though not even the intervening sonorities are purely triadic, passing added-note harmonies being created through the frequent melodic suspensions. The sequential melodic construction of the opening is developed into a more extensive type of linear intervallic pattern in bb. 29–37. Sutcliffe speaks of 'an exaggerated transition passage' here, with the descending upper voice (a^2–d^2) forming a chain of 9–5 suspensions over an extended diatonic cycle of fifths alternating seventh and ninth chords.[38] These linear elements find their culmination in the enormous descending sequence running from bb. 40 to 79. From b. 45 the IV^7–V^7 progression (closely akin to the piece's opening harmonies) is simply shifted down every diatonic scale-step across a three-octave span from c^4 to c^1 over the sequential descent of the two-bar melodic idea. By repeating the last stage as the first of the next group, Grieg rounds out the seven-part cycle into even eight-bar units. It is surely in response to this gigantic, threefold cycle that the

Example 3.15 Grieg, 'Gangar', *Lyric Pieces*, bk. V, Op. 54 No. 2

[37] The apt phrase is Grimley's (*Grieg: Music, Landscape and Norwegian Identity*, p. 77).
[38] Sutcliffe, 'Grieg's Fifth', 179.

Example 3.15 (*Continued*)

Example 3.15 (*Continued*)

Example 3.15 (*Continued*)

chromatic submediant A♭ erupts in order to counterbalance the overwhelming diatonicism of the piece.

Op. 54's 'Gangar' demonstrates the extremes to which diatonic lines may be taken: their involvement with the creation of functional added-note harmonies (almost every beat in the piece implicates extra-triadic sonorities), how such diatonic lines and fifth progressions may be mutually supportive, and their use in the systematic exploration of tessitura. Although by the time we reach the central sequence of bb. 45–68 the logic created by the linear writing overrides the initially functional tonal basis, the relatively high levels of harmonic consonance, harmonic and macroharmonic consistency,[39] and extreme use of conjunct motion directed towards hierarchical pitches nevertheless form the epitome of tonal behaviour, if the latter is understood (after Tymoczko) as arising from the interaction of such elements.

Diatonic sequences and ostinati are also a hallmark of the Op. 72 set, although here the lines are usually short and reiterative. What is most obviously missing from the language of the *Slåtter* is the chromaticism and strongly profiled descending chromatic bass lines virtually omnipresent in Op. 66 (the minor-key middle section of No. 4, 'Haugelåt Halling', is a rare exception, a reversion to a recognisably 'Griegian' voice of slipping bass chromaticism, as is a smaller instance in the centre of No. 7). Overall, the chromatic scale, and chromatically slipping sevenths chords, play no part in this set. The *Slåtter* downplay smoothness of voice leading and prohibitions on parallel movement. Instead, Grieg restrains chromaticism and preserves tonality (broadly conceived to include polytonality) through a 'primitivist' revival of fifths, root progressions (not excluding parallels and

[39] Harmonically the 'Gangar' is characterised by the predominance of seventh chords, and at a macroharmonic level by a virtual pandiatonicism.

non-parsimonious voice leading) and diatonic ostinati. As noted, there is paradoxically a greater vertical concentration on the pure harmonic consonances provided by basic intervals such as the fifth and octave, yet simultaneously an overloading of harsher dissonances against these such as major sevenths and minor ninths, or the implied tritone often created by the Lydian ♯$\hat{4}$, which creates dissonant clusters of pitches. The result is a novel and extended conception of tonality as resulting from the aggregate of numerous superimposed diatonic or modal lines (even from the harmonic overlapping of functions noted earlier in 'The Goblins' Wedding Procession'), where the level of vertical consonance may vary greatly.

Third Cycles

The enormous role played by root progressions to third-related keys in Romantic music has received sustained attention from theorists in the Neo-Riemannian tradition. Grieg's music certainly contains many elements of the triadic chromaticism typifying the nineteenth century's second practice as a constituent of its bar-by-bar harmonic language. Yet it seems noteworthy that such techniques are not among the most distinctive that Grieg developed in his later music. Chromaticism in late Grieg is more inclined to be wielded under the aegis of long-range linear processes manifested in one or more distinct lines rather than the often more ad hoc fluidity of chromatically connected chords. One evident reason for this, as explained, is that such organised principles of harmonic succession provided a supporting framework for tonal centricity. *Terzverwandschaften* and interval cycles in Grieg are indeed more likely to be used at a larger phrasal level to connect successive melodic units, either in the exposition of material or (especially in his later music) for increasing harmonic tension in central sections of pieces.

Examples of the former practice, involving third shifts applied to two- or four-bar units, have been noted already in the first theme of the Piano Concerto and in-tempo introduction to the first movement of the G minor String Quartet. The latter example is immediately suggestive of a developmental practice, in that the rising third sequence is used in the service of harmonic and expressive intensification, and creates an additional parallelism with the triadic structure of the material. A simple example from Grieg's late music, operating in three-bar units, is found in the opening of 'Resignation', the first of the seven *Stemninger*, Op. 73 (Ex. 3.16). Typical here is the outlining of the diatonic thirds of the tonic triad (E–G–B) through the individual steps in the sequence; in this entirely traditional manner, Grieg composes out a deeper tonic prolongation, again consolidating the music's harmonic grounding.

As inferred from the String Quartet, however, in formal function such techniques are particularly suited to developmental passages, where the fragmentation of larger thematic units and their swift passing

Example 3.16 Grieg, 'Resignation', *Stemninger*, Op. 73 No. 1

through a succession of keys has a long history. Fischer has pointed to the diminished triad of keys outlined near the start of the development section of the Second Violin Sonata, Op. 13 (F–A♭–b, bb. 190–204).[40] Another early example, this time of an entire equal interval cycle, is contained in the first of the four *Norwegian Dances*, Op. 35, where the developmental continuation of the opening A section presents a cycle of minor keys sequenced up a diminished seventh axis (a–c–e♭–f♯, bb. 30–47), initially in six-bar units then foreshortened to three for the latter two stages.

One of Grieg's most celebrated inspirations, 'Morning' (*Morgenstemning*) from Act IV of *Peer Gynt* (Op. 23 No. 13/Op. 46 No. 1), relies on third-relations at both small- and larger-scale levels and in presentation and developmental functions. The opening eight-bar phrase is harmonised solely by tonic and submediant chords, before a final move to the mediant initiates the second stage of a larger triadic E–G♯–B progression. After the tonic E major is regained the music pauses again on G♯ (b. 30), heard now as V/vi, leading to a harmonically more adventurous passage of second-practice chromatic slipping that goes on to dominate the central stages of the piece. Here a long-range linear descent in the bass from this G♯ to the dominant, B (b. 56), is formed out of the descending minor-third cycle G♯–F–D. The low tonic E is finally attained in b. 68 through the extension of the bass's descending line, while the final perfect cadence of bb. 78–9 is succeeded by the reiterated I–vi–I progression of the opening melody, softening classical dominant functionality with the warmth of Romantic third-relations. In this piece the diaphanous texture resulting from the reiteration of the simple opening idea through continual third shifts and smooth chromatic motion is wonderfully apposite for the evocation of dawn.

[40] Fischer, *Griegs Harmonik*, pp. 72–3.

Another good source of second-practice techniques in Grieg's oeuvre is the second piece of the Op. 73 *Moods*, 'Scherzo Impromptu' (Ex. 3.17). Most pertinent in the present context is the complete minor-third cycle (E♭–G♭–A–C–E♭) found between bb. 36 and 42, where the connecting bass line in addition outlines an ascending octatonic scale. This piece forms a neat, if hardly startling, compendium of techniques typical of Romantic triadic chromaticism, intermixed with touches of a more distinctively Griegian modality (such as the reiterated alternation between 'second practice' German sixths and 'Griegian' IV^7–i plagal cadences in bb. 10–16, the use of the minor dominant in the section following the double bar, or the humorous voice-leading parsimony that leads to the re-entry of the opening theme a semitone too low in b. 59).

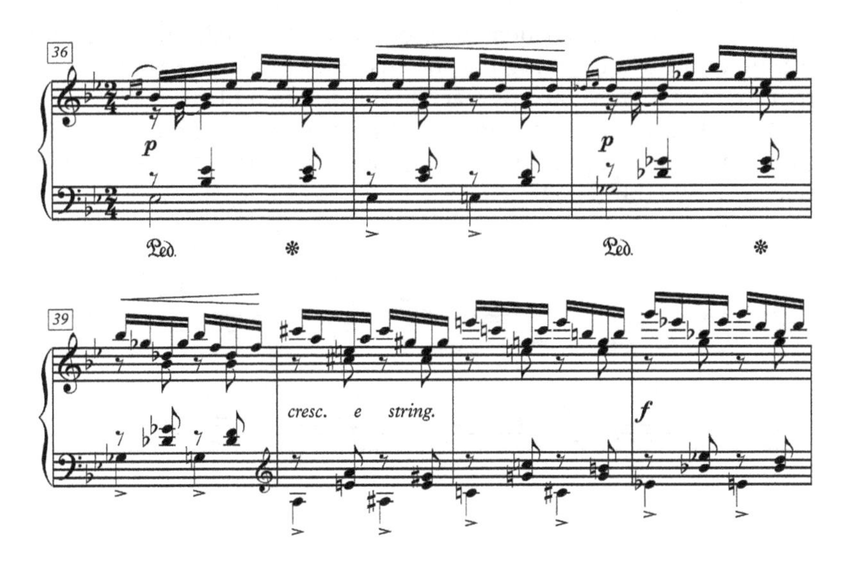

Example 3.17 Grieg, 'Scherzo Impromptu', *Stemninger,* Op. 73 No. 2

A very similar effect – one that draws on both chromatic and diatonic third cycles – may be found in 'For dine Fødder' ('At Your Feet') from the penultimate book of *Lyric Pieces,* Op. 68 No. 3. Here in the contrasting *più mosso* passage (b. 35) a diatonic third sequence leads up from the lowered mediant F via A minor and C to E minor – a tone higher than the tonic D, but easily used as a means to regain the dominant. Engaged again (bb. 55–63), the cycle now proceeds in 'chromatic' major thirds F–A–D♭, at which point the primary material is rather uncertainly taken up in a key that is again a semitone too low.

As the examples above show, Grieg at times utilises equal interval cycles of thirds that split the octave evenly in the manner much discussed in recent Neo-Riemannian theory. But this type of complete interval cycle is comparatively rare in Grieg. More common is either to have only partial statements of an equal interval cycle (for instance, presenting three stages of a minor-third cycle rather than all four that complete the cycle), or diatonic third sequences (even when continuing over an octave into a ninth or eleventh) rather than strict octave division. Belonging to the former category, for instance, is the passage in the Op. 24 *Ballade* (bb. 215–24) directly following the tonally disorientating succession of parallel seventh chords cited earlier in Ex. 1.2, where the music leads slowly back from the tritonal pole of D♭, via E, to the tonic G for a *maggiore* variation. In another example, the final 'Hjemad' ('Homewards') from the Op. 62 *Lyric Pieces*, an incomplete sequence of minor thirds rising from the dominant B becomes stuck on the tritonal harmony of F, wrenching itself back only with some effort (bb. 11–25). Similarly, the chromatically altered rising minor-third cycle opening 'Salon' from book VII of the *Lyric Pieces*, Op. 65 No. 4, only goes through three stages of the melody's sequential ascent $f\sharp^{2}$–a^{2}–$c\natural^{2}$, the harmonic underpinning of the last breaking the succession of ninth chords (E^{9}–$G\natural^{9}$) in order to make a Phrygian approach to the dominant E.

An early example of diatonic third shifts may be found in the third of the four *Humoresques*, Op. 6 No. 3 (Ex. 3.18), articulating the third cycle a–C–e–G (bb. 34–7).

Example 3.18 Grieg, *Humoresques*, Op. 6 No. 3

In the major-key central section of 'Svunne dager' ('Vanished Days'), Op. 57 No. 1, an ascending cycle of thirds leads from the tonic seventh D^{7} in dizzying sequence G^{9}–$B\flat^{9}$–D^{9}–F^{9}–$A\flat^{9}$, breaking off with a 'Tristan' half-diminished seventh as a type of musical exclamation mark (Ex. 3.19). In a manner analogous to that found later in Op. 68 No. 3 and Op. 73 No. 2, the opening theme (a major-key reformulation of that heard in the D minor outer section) then wittily emerges in D♭ – a semitone too low it soon transpires. Beyond the 'vagrancy' (as Schoenberg would put it) of the concluding half-diminished seventh, the sequence is tonally disorientating here partly because this is *not* an equal interval cycle; the listener is not guaranteed that after a certain number of stages the music will end up back on the opening pitch.

The reason why Grieg appears to prefer diatonic third cycles or merely partial chromatic ones probably lies in their being more readily accommodated into an underlying tonal syntax. Moreover, the near- (but non-) symmetrical division of the octave by thirds avoids the

Example 3.19 Grieg, 'Vanished Days', *Lyric Pieces*, bk. VI, Op. 57 No. 1

monotony of intervallic equivalence. As Tymoczko argues, with regard to both scales and harmonies, 'a bit of musical unevenness … adds musical interest by introducing a degree of variation'.[41]

For an illustration of the interaction between chromatic lines, third cycles, functional fifth progressions, scalar modulation and registral gap-filling, we may turn to the posthumously published piece usually entitled 'Wild Dance' ('Dansen går' – more literally 'The Dance goes'), EG 112. The central part of this piece's primary section (bb. 25–63) is composed of three subsections, each with its own distinct mode of pitch organisation (Ex. 3.20). Initially, a process of chromatic scalar modulation to the opening theme's diatonic $\hat{8}$–$\hat{6}$–$\hat{7}$–$\hat{5}$ motive results in a tonally decentred succession of descending major thirds followed by ascending minor thirds, thus falling overall by one chromatic step (-4 +3 -4 +3, etc.). This three-bar unit is successively raised through three minor thirds (B–D–F), bb. 25–33. Broken off prematurely on a B♭–F dyad in b. 32, for the second stage the progression is reconfigured and reversed so as to rise chromatically across the span of a fifth through alternating ascending major thirds and descending minor thirds, from B♭–D to F–A. All this is entirely motivic, an abstract development of the intervallic structure of the opening diatonic motive. Efficient voice

[41] Tymoczko, *A Geometry of Music*, pp. 122–3.

Example 3.20 Grieg, 'Wild Dance', EG 112, from *3 Piano Pieces* EG 110–112

leading in the right hand connects the third-related chords. Having reached A^7 in b. 48, the music slips chromatically down to an $F\sharp^7$ at b. 56 (thus forming one last link in the third cycle), a secondary dominant from whence functional root motion takes over to lead back to the tonic at b. 64. Despite the suggestions of wildness in the English title, in his 'Dansen går' Grieg is exploring intervallic material in an extremely systematic manner redolent (as we shall see) of other, more celebrated piano pieces from the 1890s.

Fifth Cycles and the Limits of Diatonic Tonality

As with Grieg's use of chromatic and diatonic lines, in certain pieces root motion through a perfect fifth (or fourth) becomes systematically explored beyond the limits imposed by traditional tonal progression.

Almost certainly the most extreme vision of tonal possibility in Grieg's music is 'Klokkeklang' ('Bell Ringing'), the final number of the fifth book of *Lyric Pieces* (Ex. 3.21). Sutcliffe, in his groundbreaking analysis, identifies a 'strict constructivist aspect' in Op. 54 No. 6.[42] For John Horton, similarly, this piece 'carries us right outside the classical and romantic system of harmony into regions where entirely different conceptions of chord structure and syntax hold sway'.[43] The virtually mono-textural, monothematic piano writing in 'Klokkeklang' is saturated with perfect fifths (and their inversion, the perfect fourth), to a degree unheard of before Grieg's time. The 'emancipation of sonority' inherent in Grieg's use of parallel chords of fifths does not, however, preclude the implication of an underlying harmonic structure. Indeed, Grieg's piece may be viewed as an attempt to construct tonal music operating along familiar functional lines that does without recourse to thirds, leading notes and chromatic accidentals. Nevertheless, the articulation of its tripartite form and overall arched-shaped structure relies more heavily than usual on 'secondary' parameters for its effect, such as dynamics, tessitura and differentiation of phrase rhythm, especially in the central build up to the climax at b. 49.

Grieg's initial use of perfect fifth dyads, rather than triads, immediately creates a subtle ambiguity as to harmonic identity.[44] Moritz Hauptmann had claimed that a single note may function alone as a harmony, and hence without the third to clarify triadic function a {C, G} dyad may potentially blur its implied harmony through the simultaneous incorporation of tonic and dominant functions into one entity.[45] Thus the left hand's opening ostinato alternates between dyads

[42] Sutcliffe, 'Grieg's Fifth', 165.

[43] Horton, 'Musical Personality and Style', p. 126.

[44] Triads are admittedly implicit later in the grace-note ornamentation of the melodic repetitions.

[45] Hauptmann, *The Nature of Harmony and Metre*, §65, pp. 33–4; cf. Harrison, *Harmonic Function in Chromatic Music*, p. 233.

on I and IV, suggesting a succession of plagal 'amen' cadences (tying in with the church-like connotations of the title), though the movement of the upper voice (G–c) might suggest an attempted perfect cadence, undermined by the subdominant implications of the lower voice. Moreover, in such an idiom, where each chord may simultaneously imply a given function *and* one stage further sharpwards, one finds a greater need to define the function of chords by their relative sharp- or flatward tendencies. For its fullest effect, to move to the dominant necessitates oversharpening by going one stage further than usual around the sharp-side of the cycle of fifths.[46]

To offset the bass's subdominant tendencies created through the ascending perfect fourth motion, the right hand correspondingly moves *down* in perfect fourths towards progressively more dominant areas. The result is a functional blurring between the hands to go alongside the rhythmic blurring created by syncopations and the wash of sound resulting from the depressed sostenuto pedal. In fact the two opposing tendencies exactly match Georg Capellen's designation of harmonic functions as 'Left', 'Middle' and 'Right', corresponding to the familiar Hauptmann chain of thirds articulating subdominant, tonic and dominant functions (see Fig. 3.1).[47] Conveniently in Grieg's pianistic division, the left hand oscillates between 'middle' and 'left' functions while the right hand goes increasingly 'right' (sharpwards) from the centre.

But tonality contains an imperfection. One ineliminable, original error of nature mars the diatonic system, one which Grieg's systematic construction will ruthlessly expose and exploit.

Following Sutcliffe, one might propose that the pitch organisation of the opening section of 'Klokkeklang' is constructed according to two fundamental principles.[48] First, the writing must be entirely diatonic,

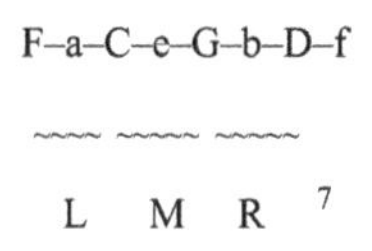

Figure 3.1 Georg Capellen's 'Left', 'Middle' and 'Right' designation of harmonic function

[46] Thus, the central section is given over to a {D, A}–{G, D} ostinato in the bass which – if the opening section is taken as prolonging I – must be understood to prolong ii, though one might also view this passage as some large-scale dominant (or 'extra-dominant') prolongation, as is typical of Grieg's central sections (complete with his habitual stacked thirds on top).

[47] L = *Linkston* or *Linksklang* (subdominant), M = *Mittelklang* (tonic), and R = *Rechtston* or *Rechtsklang* (dominant, often given as the seventh chord). See Capellen, *Die musikalische Akustik*, p. 25, *Fortschrittliche Harmonie- und Melodielehre*, p. 11.

[48] Sutcliffe, 'Grieg's Fifth' 172–3.

Example 3.21 Grieg, 'Bell Ringing', *Lyric Pieces*, bk. V, Op. 54 No. 6

Example 3.21 *(Continued)*

the notes being drawn from the C major collection (accidentals are entirely absent from the opening eighteen bars, which makes the evident movement to the dominant at b. 15 especially problematic without the possibility of modulatory tonicising). Second, both vertical formations and the horizontal organisation of pitches are based on perfect fifths or their inversional equivalent, perfect fourths. Thus, from the opening, and excluding the ornamenting acciaccaturas, the introduction of new pitches in the right hand follows the cycle of fifths (C, G (b. 1);

D (b. 3); A (b. 4); E (b. 8); B (b. 15)). The traditional phrase construction as a sixteen-bar sentence indeed plays into this constructivist conceit, whereby the presentation of the basic idea (bb. 3–6) is repeated in sequence a fourth lower as a response on the dominant (bb. 7–10), thus transposing the model one stage further round the cycle of fifths. By the double bar, Grieg has introduced all seven diatonic notes.[49] But now, to introduce another pitch is to run the two systems, formerly so mutually accommodating, into conflict with each other, and this is precisely what happens in the piece's central section.

Grieg has stopped short on the harmonic left-hand side by remaining on the first stage, F, and has gone five stages round the opposite, sharpward direction, viz.

F–C–G–D–A–E–B

The reason, clear now, is that going any further either side will either introduce an imperfect interval – the tritone, that *diabolus in musica* – consequently breaking the intervallic perfection hitherto present, or necessitate the introduction of accidentals, thus contravening the rule of diatonicism. This is what happens in b. 21, where the {B, F} dyad in the right hand forms an alien diminished sonority whose shock value within the carefully circumscribed limits of the piece can hardly be overstated.

In fact, this is not the first appearance of non-perfect vertical intervals in the piece. Even excluding the thirds given in the acciaccaturas, the putative 'modulation' to the dominant by the end of the first section has seen the unbending inflexibility of the intervallic law relaxed momentarily to allow the final note in the fifth cycle, B, to be introduced as 'wrong' sixth with G, and as a perfect fourth against E. While the latter, notwithstanding, is a perfect interval, it could easily have been presented in inverted form as a perfect fifth, and the avoidance of this latter interval here seems deliberate, almost gratuitous. Yet the soft 'added-sixth' sonority created, aiding the fragile sense of G major as a new tonal centre, does not seem dissonant, actively subversive, in the manner of the diminished fifth that materialises at b. 21.

To counterbalance the imperfection of this tritone, the dissonant note forming the new fifth, f^1, is sharpened in b. 25 to create a perfect fifth with the lower b. As Sutcliffe has observed, the solution to one problem only opens another: now accidentals have been introduced into the purity of the white-note system ('keyboard apartheid' as Sutcliffe drolly puts it).[50] The entire central section that follows is constructed from the warring conflict created between these two systems, as natural forms of the fifth are followed in turn by their sharpened kin. Yet the initial impulse for this conflict – the correction of the imperfect

[49] Indeed, including grace-notes all seven pitches have been heard sustained simultaneously in bb. 5–6, another instance of Grieg's pandiatonic added-note sonorities, similar to that seen in the earlier 'Gangar' from the same book of *Lyric Pieces*.

[50] Sutcliffe, 'Grieg's Fifth', 173.

interval – is soon left behind, as natural fifths – perfect and imperfect indiscriminately – fight it out against the chromatic additions. Typical of Grieg's ultra-constructivist design in this piece is that a system, once set up, continues to its logical consequences, even when the original cause is no longer present.

The climax of this process is reached in b. 49, the *fortississimo* dyad {E, B} set up by the steady rise in tessitura, dynamics, and a process of phrasal shortening and shifting accentual patterns. This dyad is especially significant as it contains one of the problem notes of b. 21's tritone, B, but which is now rectified by being heard as a perfect fifth with the only diatonic option open to it, a lower E. We remember now how carefully, even coyly, the composer had shunned the introduction of this remaining pitch B alongside an eminently possible perfect fifth dyad in the opening section, harmonising it with the sixth G and upper perfect fourth E rather than lower perfect fifth E. Grieg's decision to keep this event in hand is thus revealed as the result of careful strategic planning. Also in evidence is the formalistic conceit of Grieg's construction of the arch-shaped central section, for as the music subsides from the climactic attainment of this corrected perfect fifth {B, E}, the music revisits the events of its opening in reverse. Thus, in b. 53 the chromatically corrected perfect fifth on the pitches B and F is now given in flattened form {B♭, F}, rather than the sharpened instance witnessed at b. 25 {B, F♯}. Neatly, the subdominant inflection here corresponds to customary tonal behaviour, sharpening in the first half to raise tension and flattening in the second to lower it again. And to correct the original B–F diminished fifth that had caused all the problems, an F–C♯ augmented fifth, almost jestingly, overcorrects one semitone too few with one too many through the introduction of an entirely gratuitous accidental (which does nothing to rectify either of the contravened principles – that of perfect intervals or diatonicism – but merely satisfies the new palindromic order set up).

In the context of the argument pursued in this study 'Klokkeklang' provides a central example of Grieg playing with the limits of the diatonic tonal system, consciously exploring its artificiality by showing the breakdown of key elements if taken beyond a certain point. Within a piece that on one level functions as an impressionistic evocation of bell sounds filtering through the air, Grieg creates a remarkable constructivist essay in self-contained linear processes of interval and scale collection.[51] Alongside Op. 66's 'Siri Dale Visen', if any piece of Grieg's looks directly towards the systematic types of procedure that would dominate the tonally emancipated music of early twentieth-century modernity, it would be paradoxically this piece which bases itself on two of the most fundamental tenets of tonality – perfect consonant intervals and the diatonic scale as macroharmonic collection.

[51] A brief alternative reading from the perspective of scalar-subset modulation has also been given to this piece by Tymoczko, *A Geometry of Music*, pp. 341–3.

A final example in this section, returning to the themes of systematised progression, intervallic lines, the use of register and gap-fill, is 'Night Ride' (*Natligt Ridt*) Op. 73 No. 3 (Ex. 3.22). This gloomy, indeed rather menacing inspiration contained in Grieg's last piano collection sets the relation of chromatic lines and fifth progressions in a novel light, as if forming a 'linguistic battleground' between a semitonal principle and functional fifth progressions.

Implicit within the first sixteen-bar phrase are several crucial elements of the opening D minor section. Considerable focus is laid on the accented G♯ on the metrically weak third beat of b. 3, the pitch being underlined by its doubling in two octaves and through being held for the longest duration of any note in the phrase. This chromatic pitch forms an unholy tritone with the D tonic, implicitly constructed out of two minor-third steps on the diminished-seventh axis D–F–G♯ – both significant factors in the subsequent unfolding of the piece.[52] A process of gap-fill is retrospectively applied to the second of these minor-third steps (bb. 5–8). Taken together with the chromaticism resulting from the sequential repetition of this eight-bar unit over a Neapolitan sixth harmony (whose root this time implicitly forms a tritone with the dominant), the result is that by the end of the opening phrase every chromatic pitch apart from C♮ has been heard.

The prominence of the *diabolus* G♯ in b. 3 seems to constitute a musical irritant or harmonic problem, one that the enormous dominant prolongation of the central part of this outer section seeks to annul. This entire passage is formed from the slow but inexorable climb from the a in b. 17 to the a^3 in b. 85 three octaves higher, carried out almost entirely by chromatic step. An initial sixteen-bar model (bb. 17–32) ascends chromatically across successive minor third intervals, being repeated at the octave (bb. 33–48). From b. 49 the pattern breaks off, the hammered A pedal splitting into its chromatic neighbours A♭ and B♭ to form a B♭^{7} chord (b. 53). Thus, by a process of chromatic intensification in either direction the line raises its root by a semitone step, even as it reverts to its original bass tessitura. Though the dominant seventh strongly projects a need for functional resolution, this demand is denied by hammered octaves yet one step higher on B♮ back in the upper pitch range. This procedure repeats itself, registrally splitting the chromatic line into two intersecting whole-tone ascents in bass and treble. Such a process drastically slows down the rate of pitch-class ascent, but is more than counterbalanced by the increased tension resulting from the quicker rate of registral change.

Effectively the alternating dominant-seventh sonorities are functioning as passing stages in a chromatic line, arising out of the

[52] On the latter point see also Kreft, *Griegs Harmonik*, pp. 133–5. The next piece in the Op. 73 set, the charming 'Folk Tune from Valders', is (probably not coincidently) set in this enharmonic tritonal pole of A♭ major. Coincidentally or otherwise, the tritone also separates the keys of the first two pieces in the collection – E minor and B♭ major.

Example 3.22 Grieg, 'Night Ride', *Stemninger*, Op. 73 No. 3, opening section

Example 3.22 (*Continued*)

Example 3.22 (*Continued*)

semitonal slipping of individual notes in the long-range chromatic ascent. Yet their implicit harmonic functionality cannot remain contained indefinitely. From b. 67 the suppressed functional urge erupts in an extraordinary sequence of dominant sevenths sweeping up across the keyboard from the expected D^7 in a cycle of fifths G^7–C^7–F^7–$B\flat^7$–$E\flat^7$. What is most remarkable, however, is that this sixth stage in the series elides with the $e\flat^3$ in the upper line leading from the $c\sharp^3$ of b. 66, which should have followed the low D^7. In one stroke the released functional fifth behaviour restores the split chromatic registral lines to the correct upper tessitura implied by the large-scale linear ascent.

Continuing on to the expected $e\natural^3$ the reengaged chromatic line now skips a semitonal step on $f\natural^3$, becoming stuck between $e\natural^3$ and $f\sharp^3$, as if frantically searching for this missing stage. C♯ minor and F♯ chords alternate *agitato* before this $f\natural^3$ is at last found in b. 83: there follows the long-anticipated climax of the section, a *fff feroce* outburst of the 'Grieg motive' cascading down from the a^3 peak of the linear ascent. As in 'Klokkeklang' earlier, this tension gradually dissipates through fragmentation of the primary theme. Diatonic chords on B♭ and G minor, reinterpreting the common tonic pitch of D, diffuse the chromatic minor thirds of the theme preceding them, before a *pianissimo* restatement of the opening theme rounds off the arch-shaped design as it had started.

'Night Ride' engages with the now-familiar themes of linear directionality, pitch centricity, register and gap-fill in Grieg's music. What is most fascinating about this particular work, however, is the pitting of systematic interval cycles against one another – chromatic lines organised in minor-third segments versus cycles of functional dominant sevenths – and even more intriguingly how the latter is able to grow out of and displace the former, before becoming the agent of its eventual restoration.

Tritones and The Limits of Systematised Intervallic Succession

Moving beyond the perfection of fourths and fifths, systematic use of the most basic equal octave division – the tritone – as a principle of harmonic succession appears difficult. Admittedly the voice leading, in theory, could be smooth between the first and fifth scale degrees of each chord (if perfect fifths are acceptable inverted into their quartal brethren), and seventh chords on tritonal roots are famously blessed with close voice-leading possibilities, but after one stage there is nowhere to go in the cycle except back to the opening harmony. Tritonal organisation, by itself, scarcely escapes from the ring of monotony. Grieg comes close to this in the 'Scene with the Bøyg' from *Peer Gynt* (Op. 23 No. 9), where an initial long-held B♭ is juxtaposed with E♮ to form a tritone; this done, however, the interval can merely be raised in sequence through semitonal step (a procedure that has left several critics underwhelmed). Thus tritone progressions are normally used for short expressive effect, either in alternation with other classes of interval or its status as harmonic *non sequitur* exploited as a type of musical exclamation mark. In such a form, Grieg is very fond of its expressive potential: examples of direct tritone alternation can found in the early 'Bridal Procession Passes By' (*Brudefølget drar forbi*) from the *Scenes from Folklife*, Op. 19 No. 2, and 'March of the Trolls' (*Troldtog*) Op. 54 No. 3 (Exs 3.23 and 3.24).

Example 3.23 Grieg, 'Bridal Procession Passes By', *Scenes from Folklife*, Op. 19 No. 2

Example 3.24 Grieg, 'March of the Trolls', *Lyric Pieces*, bk. V, Op. 54 No. 3

Similar in effect, if harmonically simpler, is the alternation of an illusory E major harmony with an obdurate low B♭ dominant in the late *Lyric Piece* 'Little Troll' Op. 71 No. 3 (bb. 48–53), or the converse interruption of a G⁷ dominant with ominous octave D♭s in the fifth piece of the set, 'Halling' (bb. 53–60) – a feature which results in a chain of alternating tritones and perfect fourths in the piece's coda. In fact the tritone progression appears with increased frequency in Grieg's late piano works. As these last examples demonstrate, a phrase may end up a tritone away from its intended harmonic goal, resulting in a wry jolt (other instances include 'She Dances', Op. 57 No. 5, bb. 66–8, and 'Valse mélancolique', Op. 68 No. 6, bb. 20–1), or the tritone can emerge as a local disruptive element, a malign presence undermining a large dominant preparation (as in the fourth of the *Stemninger*, 'Studie (Hommage à Chopin)', bb. 34–8).

Yet this progression may also evoke quite a different mood: in the 'Bådnlåt' ('Cradle Song') from the Op. 68 book of *Lyric Pieces*, a pronounced cycle of fifths progression halts on a secondary dominant ninth (F♯⁹, b. 24); rather than proceeding through the expected dominant to the return of the opening theme in the tonic (b. 28), Grieg softly introduces a miraculous C⁹ chord, a tritone removed, which, functioning as a German sixth, slips to the tonic $^6_4$. Prominent tritone motion interspersed with a mediant shift also contributes to the languidly non-functional 'Summer Evening' (*Sommeraften*), Op. 71 No. 2 (Ex. 3.25),

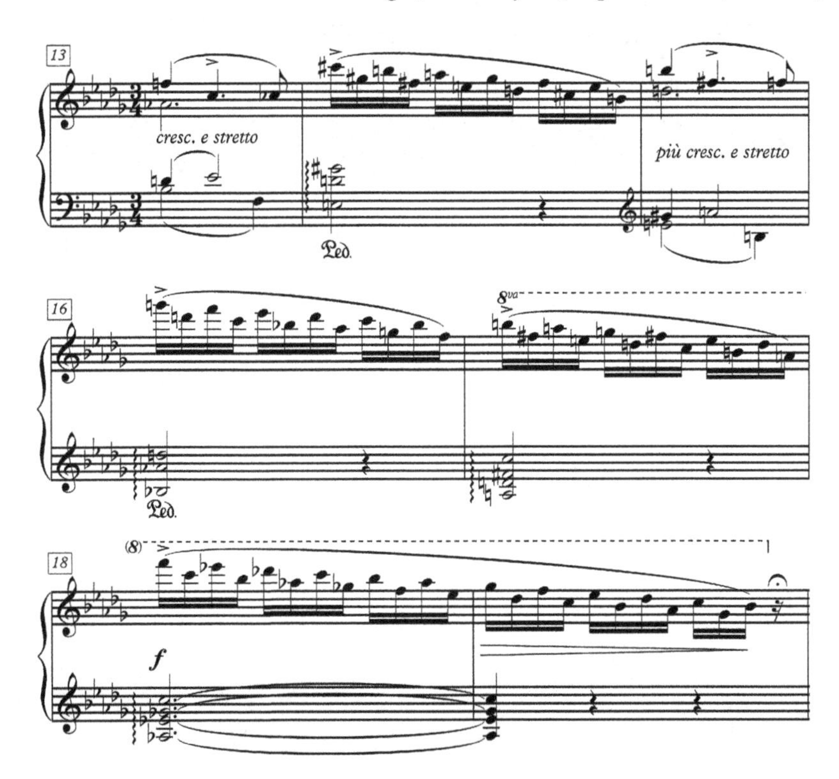

Example 3.25 Grieg, 'Summer Evening', *Lyric Pieces*, bk. X, Op. 71 No. 2

a particularly colouristic use replete with filigree arabesques decorating the progression).

Elsewhere (as already illustrated in several examples), tritonal root progressions may arise naturally as the one imperfect stage in diatonic cycles of fifths (as, correspondingly, a semitonal root progression may be altered to emphasise the imperfect fifth in the bass, as seen earlier in 'Det syng', Ex. 1.6). However, in none of these above instances may Grieg's use accurately be described as systematic.

In both 'Bell Ringing' and 'Night Ride', the tritone appears as a *diabolus in musica* – one to be shunned in the former, a darkly motivating force in the latter. But on rare occasions, as in 'Cradle Song', it might also be used to magical effect. Possibly at the very end of Op. 71 No. 4 we might grant the composer moments of 'free succession' in Fischer's apt choice of phrase (Ex. 3.26).[53] Coming at the end of an impressionistic miniature in a radiant B major in which the tonic has been heard preceded by a subdued minor dominant, the simple *pianissimo* alternation of the tonic with an incomprehensible, perfect F major seems a breath from another world. What abstract intervallic qualities remain become absorbed into a purely colouristic practice.

Example 3.26 Grieg, 'Peace of the Woods', *Lyric Pieces*, bk. X, Op. 71 No. 4

[53] Fischer, *Griegs Harmonik*, pp. 80ff.

Conclusion

Nature and nationalism

> Thank God the combinations [of harmonies] are inexhaustible in number ... everybody may then find new side paths for himself leading to ever new perspectives on regions never entered before.[1]

On the face of it, the sentiments expressed above sound as if they might come from a figure committed to musical pluralism, to the liberal expansion of the realm of harmony that would potentially decentre any hegemonic mainstream narrative. In fact, they come, not from Grieg or any contemporary theorist informed by post-modern concerns, but from that arch-constructor of Germanic musical supremacy, Hugo Riemann. Despite Riemann making this claim at the close of his early *Musikalische Syntaxis*, as recent scholars have observed, Riemann saw harmony – or his own theorisation of it – as both a conserving force and a notion adequate to ensure the dominance of German musical practice for the foreseeable future.[2] Insofar as Riemann sought to control the subsequent course of compositional history, he obviously failed. Yet the tensions resulting from such regulatory endeavours have nonetheless been felt strongly throughout the subsequent century of music theory and historiography.

Grieg had an uneasy relationship with Riemann. Although the critic had been favourably disposed towards some of his early German *Lieder*, a comment added to the entry on Grieg in the fourth edition of the *Musik-Lexikon* from 1894 provoked friction with the composer. Though praising the poetic imagination of Grieg's music, Riemann adds that 'it is to be regretted [Grieg] imposed upon himself the limitations of national characteristics and instead of using the musical world-language speaks more or less a local dialect!'[3] The peripheralisation of Grieg's music through the fact of its purported Norwegianness and implicit

[1] Hugo Riemann, *Musikalische Syntaxis* (Leipzig: Breitkopf & Härtel, 1877), p. 120, trans. by Alexander Rehding in *Hugo Riemann and the Birth of Modern Musical Thought* (Cambridge, Cambridge University Press, 2003), p. 105.

[2] As Rehding notes, 'Riemann's theory of harmony, the notion of a systematic logic in music' was 'a bastion against historical change' – 'harmony is depicted as a force independent of history, as a timeless, unchanging structure'. *Hugo Riemann and the Birth of Modern Musical Thought*, p. 110.

[3] Hugo Riemann, *Musik-Lexikon*, fourth edition (Leipzig: Max Hesse Verlag, 1894), p. 399 ('es ist daher zu bedauern, dass er sich selbst die Beschrankung nationaler Charakteristik auserlegt und statt der musikalischen Weltsprache mehr oder weniger einen lokalen Dialekt spricht!').

identification of music's 'world-language' with that of Germany could not be clearer.

But metaphors are dangerous. The movement from one term or conceptual terrain to another, once introduced, proliferates and may easily slip out of control, the analogy taking on new, sometimes diametrically opposed meanings. One of the aims of this monograph is to argue that, for Grieg at least, the realm of harmony was as Riemann claims one of inexhaustible richness, and what is more (as Riemann unsuspectingly implies) that by uncovering and exploring its previously unchartered, even peripheral regions, Grieg is in fact laying greater claim on possessing a truly world-language than a music emanating from within the narrowly circumscribed borders of Riemann's Wilhelmine Germany. Perhaps, indeed, the familiar space of Riemann's metaphorical terrain is inadequate for encapsulating the multiplicity of harmonic techniques available to Grieg. The geometry of dreamworlds rarely conforms to that of quotidian normality: a different, higher-dimensional Riemannian geometry (more Bernhard than Hugo as it were) may be needed as a paradigm.

As set out in the introduction to this study, there are many different aspects to Grieg's harmonic practice. Functional fifth progressions, second-practice triadic chromaticism, modality and scalar modulation, extended supra-triadic tonal harmony and the systematisation of lines and interval cycles all belong to the rich array of techniques Grieg utilises in his later music. What is particularly interesting theoretically are certain artful, methodical ways of employing these – the systematic exploration of added-note tetrachords in 'Gjætle-Bekken' from both functional and chromatic perspectives; the blurring of harmonic and scalar collections in 'Ola Valley' and subtle reinterpretation of traditional schemata through scalar inflection; the diverse processes of scalar modulation in 'The Brook', 'Dream Vision' and 'Wild Dance'; or the use of chromatic lines and semitonal transposition of seventh chords in a number of works from the 1890s where functional implications are almost entirely negated. In the extraordinary 'Klokkeklang' tonal elements, taken beyond certain limits, destroy the simplicity of the initial system, but create ever-richer layers of music following new, extended tonal grammars. Conversely, in the 'Gangar' from the same set of *Lyric Pieces*, the massive registral descent in the centre shows how diatonic sequences can be extended indefinitely (at least until the basic parameter of register runs out); the chromatic incursion of A♭ at the end comes almost as a relief.[4] Finally, Op. 73's 'Night Ride' counterpoises chromatic lines and minor-third cycles with that most-functional of harmonies, the dominant seventh, to create a porous interface between tonal and more atonal principles in the service of a broader pitch centricity.

[4] Grimley highlights this same point in his consideration of this piece, *Grieg: Music, Landscape and Norwegian Identity*, p. 77.

In all these procedures, Grieg may be witnessed enriching and widening particular elements of tonal practice, sometimes in isolation, on other occasions in complex interaction. Just as Hyer argues that the historical concept of tonality is a polyvalent entity, so as exemplified in Grieg's music a plurality of approaches to harmonic tonality were available to composers by the late nineteenth century. Overall there is little sense of a single practice for tonal harmony at this time, but rather a multitude of ways of playing with diverse harmonic elements and techniques that constitute tonal behaviour. Thus conceived, familiar narratives of the decline of functional harmony and its superseding by chromaticism appear too simplistic. Neither do the refinements brought by Neo-Riemannian conceptualisations of a second practice account for the full diversity of Grieg's harmonic techniques: there is more than simply a first (functional) and second (chromatic triadic) practice present behind Grieg's music. The notion of an extended tonal Franco-Russian tradition (as contrasted with a 'chromatic' Austro-German heritage), suggested by Jim Samson long ago and taken up in Tymoczko's notion of an opposing 'scalar' tradition, is useful,[5] but there is still more to Grieg's harmonic language than can be reduced to any of these categories.

As demonstrated, the composer utilises several techniques for restraining chromaticism, but yet there remains plenty of chromaticism within Grieg's music, some of it quite pronounced. Chromatic succession may appear highly systematised, but so too may other scalar or intervallic modes of organisation. There is still a strong sense of underlying functionality, even when contained in the new tonal grammars of the *Slåtter*, alongside a conscious exploration of its limits, such as is found in 'Klokkeklang'. Modality and multiple forms of the minor scale may be freely drawn upon, and the articulatory force of dominant-tonic polarity is frequently replaced by plagal movement. Benestad and Schjelderup-Ebbe speak rightly of Grieg's 'unerring ability' in his harmonic style 'to create a synthesis out of the most diverse elements which fit together so well as to form a unified whole'.[6] 'Tonality', at least by the end of the nineteenth century, could be viewed more accurately as an eclectic constellation of practices and compromises, some of these being partially (though nevertheless incompletely) based on 'natural' properties. Grieg is just quite open in exploring tonality's diversity and constructedness in an unselfconsciously radical manner.

Indeed, one could argue that the very nature of Grieg's music – his characteristic scale, formal designs and phrase-syntax – particularly concentrates the impact of these harmonic qualities. Grieg has

[5] An interesting (if neglected) earlier formulation of this division is also found in Rudolph Réti's distinction between the customary 'harmonic tonality' of Western common practice and a 'melodic tonality' whose development by Debussy prefigures what Réti terms 'pantonality' (*Tonality, Atonality, Pantonality: A Study of Some Trends in Twentieth Century Music* (London: Barries and Rockliff, 1958), pp. 7–26).

[6] Benestad and Schjelderup-Ebbe, *Edvard Grieg: The Man and the Artist*, p. 404.

habitually been relegated to the second division of great composers owing chiefly to his reputation as a miniaturist, a *petit maître* comfortable only with the small-scale designs of the piano miniature, song, orchestral character piece or nationally inspired dance. (The Piano Concerto forms the honourable exception, and even this work's success is normally explained by its modelling on Schumann's concerto; other extended designs such as the String Quartet were, until recently, routinely patronised for their supposed formal weaknesses or textual novelty.) There is no succession of monumental symphonic utterances that grace the genre, no monolithic opera tetralogy lasting days. In their place, we have only an accomplished but disowned youthful Symphony in C minor and fragments for the unrealised opera on *Olav Trygvason*. Unlike other masters of the smaller-scale medium such as Chopin, his piano music's customary association with the amateur market (created above all from the enormous success of the ten books of *Lyric Pieces*) has prevented Grieg from occupying a central place in the professional repertoire which might otherwise allow his promotion to the upper division among piano aficionados. The nineteenth-century piano repertoire is poorer but no less conceivable without Grieg. Rikard Nordraak, in describing his first meeting with Grieg, criticises the composer in terms that make for familiar reading: 'He tries too hard to find the great within the small and often elevates the latter at the expense of the former'.[7] But this overlooks one crucial point, for in terms of harmony at least the small is particularly suited to Grieg's unique musical qualities.

In considering the question of miniaturism it is necessary to bear in mind the relation between form and syntax – how a work's larger structure and the nature of its small-scale harmonic syntax, especially the degree to which chromaticism may be present, are often mutually dependent. The propensity for one type of construction – be it melodic gift, harmonic inventiveness, or formal sophistication – will undoubtedly have an effect on the other dimensions of the music.[8] Different parameters are interlinked. In Grieg, the response to the charge of miniaturist lies to a considerable degree in the very capacity of his relatively simple forms and quadratic melodic phrases to afford a more exploratory use of harmony within them. The generally four-square nature of his phrasing and the schematic formal moulds of Grieg's sonata style or ternary designs are the reciprocal side of a harmonic syntax which evinces greater flexibility at the small-scale level.

As a consequence, the nature of Grieg's phrase-syntax is particularly suited to focusing attention on the harmonic component of his

[7] Ibid., p. 46.

[8] A point well made by Horton, 'Musical Personality and Style', pp. 121ff. As Schoenberg, in his *Fundamentals of Musial Composition*, similarly argues, the complex harmony that grew up in the nineteenth century was necessarily counteracted by simplification in other planes (*Fundamentals of Musial Composition*, ed. Gerald Strang and Leonard Stein (London: Faber and Faber, 1967), p. 31).

music. A relatively conservative phrase structure is counterbalanced by an often radical development in the harmonic field. Sometimes, indeed, the harmonic treatment constitutes the primary interest in the music, the melodic voice being little more than a thread upon which the harmonies are strung (as exemplified in some of Grieg's more adventurous folksong arrangements, or other character pieces of his based on folk material).[9]

Yet despite the radical nature of his harmonic achievements, one might still foresee possible criticism aimed at Grieg's music from a hard-line modernist perspective, in that in terms of the 'state of musical material' his music's harmonic development is not matched by a comparable advancement in other parameters. The foreshadowing of the twentieth-century impressionism of Debussy or the primitivism of Bartók or Stravinsky is achieved in Grieg alongside a conservatism of structure and, often as not, an apparently regressive return to pre-tonal, modal folk idioms. This criticism, however, relies on the presumption that there is a single historical stream of development, and accordingly on determining a historical yardstick to be drawn from this – assumptions, argued earlier, that appear distinctly rash. We need to get away from the well-worn idea of a singular historical stream of harmonic practice (as is suggested by Daniel Grimley's tacit criticism of Dahlhaus in his reading of the modernist imperative behind Op. 66's 'Siri Dale Visen').[10] As Jim Samson remarks, 'whatever interpretation Schoenberg may have placed on the historical significance of his own earlier music and of his subsequent break with tonality, a close inspection of the impulses involved in tonal decline would prompt many of us to question, or at least qualify, the notion of any single "mainstream" development towards atonality'.[11]

Thus historical and cultural relativism with respect to the development of tonal harmony provides us with a better chance of appreciating Grieg's musical achievement than theories reflecting the traditional linear narrative of harmonic development. Still, Grieg's views and practice do seem to imply a mild paradox, at least set against the conventional wisdom of Germanocentric historiography, in that while a historically and culturally relativistic perspective certainly enables a more insightful account of the richness and multifaceted nature of his harmonic usage, the composer himself seems to have held strong, albeit often inchoate, beliefs in the natural basis of harmony. (One should also be

[9] A prime example of such melodic simplicity and the corresponding musical intensification through harmonic means is given by 'Homesickness' (*Hjemve*), Op. 57 No. 6 (said by Röntgen to have been inspired by the three notes of a goat-horn tune heard during a 1891 trip to Jotunheim), or the 'Folk-Melody', Op. 73 No. 4, which derives much of its interest and considerable charm from Grieg's harmonic elaboration of a simple conjunct figure (generically akin to a *kulokk*) based on the first four scale degrees in A♭ major.

[10] Grimley, *Grieg: Music, Landscape and Norwegian Identity*, pp. 101 and 108.

[11] Samson, *Music in Transition*, p. 60.

wary of simply dismissing the Germanocentric narrative as mere ideology, since as a historical reality it was something that Grieg's views also orientated themselves around.[12])

For all the dubious appeal to natural essence and nationhood, however, there need not be a contradiction in Grieg's views. As Grimley surmises, Grieg appears to have held an atavistic doctrine, seeking truth in a movement back to the mountains of Norway, his country's nature and folk.[13] In the composer's statements on the secret mysteries of music and the natural inspiration behind the audacious harmonies used in Op. 66 we may perceive a belief in a more primal essence, something lost by time and obscured by the narrow stream of Germanic practices that wrongly lay claim on total musical hegemony, which may be renewed by drawing upon other, uncorrupted practices. Truth, as Romantic theories of ethnicity, language and nationhood would stress, is relative to a specific culture.[14] If the essence of harmony and his music's connexion with his native folk music were still self-confessedly an enigma to Grieg, this might suggest that tonality's natural basis is something which cultural constructions – be they Norwegian, Danish or German – may ever only approximate in their different, contingent ways. To this extent, Grieg's achievement is both national and yet transcends the merely national archetype that has for so long been inextricably bound up with it. As he avowed barely a year before his death, 'Music that is lastingly good, be it in any case ever so national, rises high above the merely national level. It is cosmopolitan.'[15]

[12] Grimley pertinently comments that the 'sense of peripheralisation, of marginalisation from a perceived mainstream, is as strong as the sense of local identity' in some of Grieg's written statements (*Grieg: Music, Landscape and Norwegian Identity*, p. 115). Indeed, in some of his journalistic pieces Grieg refers to his native Norway, half-ironically, as 'Ultima Thule', a land lying 'far north' of the civilised world (*Artikler og taler*, pp. 125, 207/*Diaries, Articles, Speeches*, pp. 256, 199).

[13] Grimley, *Grieg: Music, Landscape and Norwegian Identity*, p. 116.

[14] This is aligning Grieg with the more inclusive, Herderian version of Romantic nationalism outlined by Richard Taruskin, 'Nationalism', *The New Grove Dictionary of Music and Musicians*, ed. Stanley Sadie, 29 vols. (London: Macmillan, 2001), vol. 17, pp. 689–706. Grieg's cultural relativism became ever more pronounced with age. In a letter to Frants Beyer of 10 March 1890, the composer emphasises the inescapable variability of artistic ideals and impossibility of claiming one belief is definitive for all peoples and ages: 'can't those people understand there exists no *absolute* truth[?] When each one seeks the truth in his own way, everything is well' ('Kan de Mennesker da ikke forstå, at noget *absolute* Sandhed findes ikke. Når Enhver søger Sandhed på sin Måde, så blir Alt godt'; *Brev til Frants Beyer 1872–1907*, ed. Finn Benestad and Bjarne Kortsen (Oslo: Universitetsforlaget, 1993), p. 153/*Letters to Colleagues and Friends*, p. 62). Similarly, in the last decade or so of his life he repeatedly underscores his distaste for a narrow, exclusive brand of nationalism: 'to be a chauvinist is not to be Norwegian!' he holds (letter to Hans Lien Brækstad, 23 February 1898, *Brev*, vol. I, p. 120/*Letters*, p. 155).

[15] Grieg, diary entry for 30 May 1906 ('Den Musik som duger, den er ialtfald om aldrig så national, dog højt hævet over det blot nationale Niveau. Den er kosmopolitisk'), in *Dagbøker 1865, 1866, 1905, 1906 og 1907*, ed. Finn Benestad (Bergen: Bergen Offentlige Bibliotek, 1993), p. 144, translation modified from *Diaries, Articles, Speeches*, p. 137.

Ultimately, then, this study might be read as arguing for a post-nationalist understanding of Grieg's work. All his life the composer, by his own account, was fascinated by the realm of harmony. It is as if this enchanted dreamworld formed a limitless realm for exploration, one whose obscure depths could be forever extended, whose undreamt-of harmonic possibilities always enriched, whose elements reconfigured and recombined. Hence, there exists such a plurality of approaches to harmony in his music, some pieces concentrating more single-mindedly on a specific technical aspect than others. And, despite granting the historical reality of Germanocentric music-historical narratives and the composer's own, uneasy participation in these, if we grant that both tonality and late-nineteenth-century harmonic practice are a constellation of divergent elements and techniques, then should not the very diversity of Grieg's practice and distance from a central Austro-German chromatic tradition, rather than being marked as peripheral, be held up instead as a model of tonal music in all its 'messy diversity' and cosmopolitan multiplicity?[16]

Epilogue: Lost in the Mountains

In a letter of 1905 to his close friend, Frants Beyer, Grieg reveals

> when I was your age ... I did not yet feel, in relation to nature's towering mountains, the sense of sadness that has since cast itself over my outlook .... For me, mysticism has always prevented jubilation from taking the upper hand. I could indeed rejoice inwardly over the free life. But nature itself? Face to face with nature I stood in silent reverence and awe as if before God himself.
>
> Certainly I love science's urge to clarity. But the mystical attracts me nonetheless...[17]

Coming at the end of one of Grieg's richest explorations of harmony, the magnificent, enormously articulated plagal cadence closing 'I Wander Deep in Thought' would make a fitting conclusion to the entire Op. 66 set, matching the fragile status of the plagal cadence so dearly sought in the opening 'Kulokk' and its wonderfully expressive articulation to

Earlier, in 1889, the composer had likewise felt moved to pen a 'Cosmopolitan Credo' to the Danish periodical *Musikbladet*.

[16] As Finck long ago acutely remarked, 'When a German fancies that his country owns the "world language" in music, one may pardon him, for national vanity is a universal folly ... Dialect signifies a provincial way of speaking a language. What is Norway a province of, musically or otherwise? ... At one time, not so very long ago, Italian was the "world language" in music...in all probability they considered German music a mere "dialect"'. Henry T. Finck, *Grieg and his Music* (New York: John Lane, 1910), pp. 126–7.

[17] Grieg, letter to Frants Beyer, 4 August 1905 ('at da jeg var på Din Alder (altså 54), da følte jeg i Forhold til den store Fjeldnatur endnu ikke den Vemod som siden også har lagt sig over mit Syn .... For mig har Mystiken altid hindret Jubelen fra at tage Overhånd. Det fri Liv kunde jeg nok indvendig juble over. Men Naturen selv? Overfor den stod jeg i taus ærbødighed og ærefrygt som foran Gud selv .... Ganske vist: Jeg elsker Videnskabens Trang til Klarhed. Men det Mystiske drager mig alligevel'), *Brev til Frants Beyer*, p. 328, translation modified from *Letters to Colleagues and Friends*, pp. 96–7.

close 'In Ola Valley, in Ola Lake'. Those who have accompanied Grieg throughout his travels across the dreamworld of harmony experience a progression from the natural call of the opening number, through the pictures from folk-life of numerous folksongs, by turns calm, boisterous and tragic, to an almost religious fervour – a movement, as it were, from nature, through life, to God. Yet one piece still remains in this collection. The effect of the concluding G minor 'Gjendine's Lullaby', Op. 66 No. 19, is strongly anticlimactic, decidedly lowering the emotional temperature. We revert again to a 'typical' Op. 66 number, a small-scale, unassuming, somewhat bleak minor-tinted arrangement. Gone is the richness and expressive fulsomeness of 'Jeg går i tusind tanker' and its elevated tone.[18]

Might this final piece be a memory for Grieg? This is the one folksong in the collection that the composer notated himself, capturing it during his 1891 tour of Jotunheimen where, deeply moved, he heard it from a young herding girl Gjendine Slålien at Skogadalsbøen. Did the lullaby denote not only the peace of sleep but that of oncoming death for the aging composer, just as Gjætle Brook at this same time offered an ambiguous homecoming for *Haugtussa*'s protagonist, Veslemøy? The overall implications for the Op. 66 set, specifically its larger expressive trajectory, certainly seem significant. There can be no religious fulfilment, *ad astra* telos, within this collection. This suggestion, articulated by the hymnlike splendour of No. 18, is undercut by the subsequent movement back into nature in No. 19: not a hostile one, but nevertheless one that possesses a bleak or indifferent quality.

If anything, the effect is even darker at the close of Grieg's final piano collection, the *Stemninger* Op. 73. In the seventh and final piece, 'Mountaineer's Song', a number again set in a bare G minor, the composer's use of the modal $\sharp\hat{4}$ inflection and textural *Klang* leaves its ghostly echoes reverberating around the mountain peaks: in Kathleen Dale's marvellous description, the listener is 'chased by echoing canons until the volume of tone gradually amassed seems to reverberate around the mountain-tops before eventually dying away into the stillness of vast spaces'.[19] Again, we are taken back into nature, a wider and crucial trope within Grieg's work, as Grimley's important reading of *Den Bergtekne* (literally 'the one taken into the mountains'), Op. 32, so powerfully demonstrates.[20] Despite the bleak chromaticism of Grieg's setting, in the earlier piece entitled 'In Folk-Style', Op. 63 No. 1, the benediction of that final, plagal cadence is granted, just as it is in the first number of Op. 66, but the ultimate conclusions to both the Op. 66 and Op. 73 sets are far more equivocal. As the composer withdraws

[18] Gone, too, is the erstwhile tonal symmetry of the set: had the collection ended with No. 18 it would have closed back in D major, the key of the opening 'Kulokk'.

[19] Kathleen Dale, 'The Piano Music', p. 57.

[20] Grimley, *Grieg: Music, Landscape and Norwegian Identity*, pp. 79–86.

from the scene, nature, landscape, and the folk who for their allotted cycle take their entrances and exits against it, still remain, unaffected.

Such thoughts might offer the would-be theorist cause for reflection on the contingent nature of his or her enterprise in coming to an ultimate understanding of Griegian harmony. If tonality's hidden nature can only be imperfectly grasped by the cultural constructions of compositional technique, it is hardly surprising if a derivative analytical method – a second-level activity – is at best hermeneutic. A constant gap or disparity remains between mankind and nature, between composer and folk, between theorist and music's enigmatic harmony. Like the hidden harmony of nature Grieg sensed behind his native country's folk-melodies, like the relation of the tonal system to natural harmonic properties, like our understanding of tonality itself, we may approximate it, but never fully realise it. However we try to explore it, however we try to deepen our understanding of this dream-realm, there will always remain more to discover.

Bibliography

Bailey, Robert: 'An Analytical Study of the Sketches and Drafts', in *Richard Wagner: Prelude and Transfiguration from 'Tristan und Isolde' (Norton Critical Score)*, ed. Robert Bailey (New York: W. W. Norton, 1985).

Bass, Richard: 'Half-Diminished Functions and Transformations in Late Romantic Music', *Music Theory Spectrum*, 23 (2001), 41–60.

Benestad, Finn and Schjelderup-Ebbe, Dag: *Edvard Grieg: Mennesket og kunstneren* (Oslo: Aschehoug, 1980), trans. William H. Halverson and Leland B. Sateren as *Edvard Grieg: The Man and the Artist* (Gloucester: Alan Sutton, 1988).

—— *Edvard Grieg: Chamber Music: Nationalism, Universality, Individuality* (Oslo: Scandinavian University Press, 1993).

Bernstein, David W.: 'Georg Capellen's Theory of Reduction: Radical Harmonic Theory at the Turn of the Twentieth Century', *Journal of Music Theory*, 37 (1993), 85–116.

Bjørndal, Arne: *Norsk folkemusikk* (Bergen: Nord- og Midhordland sogelag, 1952).

Boretz, Benjamin: 'Meta-Variations: Studies in the Foundations of Musical Thought' (PhD diss., Princeton University, 1970).

Capellen, Georg: *Die musikalische Akustik als Grundlage der Harmonik und Melodik* (Leipzig: C.F. Kahnt Nachfolger, 1902).

—— *Die Freiheit oder Unfreiheit der Töne und Intervalle als Kriterium der Stimmführung nebst einem Anhang: Grieg-Analysen als Bestätigungsnachweis und Wegweiser der neuen Musiktheorie* (Leipzig: C.F. Kahnt Nachfolger, 1904).

—— *Fortschrittliche Harmonie- und Melodielehre* (Leipzig: C.F. Kahnt Nachfolger, 1908).

Carley, Lionel (ed.): *Grieg and Delius: A Chronicle of Their Friendship in Letters* (London: Marion Boyars, 1993).

Carley, Lionel: *Edvard Grieg in England* (Woodbridge: The Boydell Press, 2006).

Childs, Adrian P.: 'Moving Beyond Neo-Riemannian Triads: Exploring a Transformational Model for Seventh Chords', *Journal of Music Theory*, 42 (1998), 181–93.

Clark, Suzannah and Rehding, Alexander (eds.): *Music Theory and Natural Order from the Renaissance to the Early Twentieth Century* (Cambridge: Cambridge University Press, 2001).

Cohn, Richard: 'Square Dances with Cubes', *Journal of Music Theory*, 42 (1998), 283–96.

—— 'Weitzmann's Regions, My Cycles, and Douthett's Dancing Cubes', *Music Theory Spectrum*, 22 (2000), 89–103.

—— *Audacious Euphony: Chromatic Harmony and the Triad's Second Nature* (New York: Oxford University Press, 2012).

Dahlhaus, Carl: *Nineteenth-Century Music*, trans. J.B. Robinson (Berkeley and Los Angeles: University of California Press, 1989).

Dale, Kathleen: 'The Piano Music', in Gerald Abraham (ed.), *Edvard Grieg: A Symposium* (London: Lindsay Drummond, 1948), pp. 45–70.

Dinslage, Patrick: 'Edvard Griegs Jugendwerk im Spiegel seiner Leipziger Studienjahre', *Svensk tidskrift för musikforskning*, 78 (1996), 25–50.

Douthett, Jack and Steinbach, Peter: 'Parsimonious Graphs: A Study in Parsimony, Contextual Transformations, and Modes of Limited Transposition', *Journal of Music Theory*, 42 (1998), 241–63.

Eriksen, Asbjørn Ø.: 'Griegian Fingerprints in the Music of Frederick Delius (1862–1934)', paper presented at the International Grieg Society Conference, Bergen 30 May 2007, http://www.griegsociety.org/default.asp?kat=1009&id=4515&sp=2.

Findeisen, Peer: 'Ethnofolkloristische Anmerkungen zu Griegs Klavierzyklus *19 norske folkeviser* op. 66', in Ekkehard Kreft (ed.), *Bericht des 1. Deutschen Edvard-Grieg-Kongresses* (Altenmedingen: Hildegard-Junker-Verlag, 1996), pp. 135–51.

—— 'Naturmystik als Kern der Einheit von Ton und Wort in Griegs Liederzyklus *Haugtussa*, op. 67', *Studia Musicologica Norvegica*, 25 (1999), 124–43.

Finck, Henry Theophilus: *Grieg and His Music* (New York: John Lane, 1910).

Fischer, Kurt von: *Griegs Harmonik und die nordländische Folklore* (Bern and Leipzig: Paul Haupt, 1938).

Fog, Dan, Grinde, Kirsti and Norheim, Øyvind (eds.), *Edvard Grieg, Thematisch-Bibliographisches Werkverzeichnis* (Frankfurt, Leipzig, London and New York: Henry Litolffs Verlag/Peters, 2008).

Foster, Beryl: *The Songs of Edvard Grieg* (Aldershot: Scholar Press, 1990).

—— *Edvard Grieg: The Choral Music* (Aldershot: Ashgate, 1999).

Gjerdingen, Robert O.: *Music in the Galant Style* (New York: Oxford University Press, 2007).

Gollin, Edward: 'Some Aspects of Three-Dimensional *Tonnetze*', *Journal of Music Theory*, 42 (1998), 195–206.

Gollin, Edward and Rehding, Alexander (eds.): *The Oxford Handbook of Neo-Riemannian Music Theories* (New York: Oxford University Press, 2011).

Grainger, Percy [Aldridge]: 'Personal Recollections of Grieg', *Musical Times*, 48/777 (November 1907), 720.

—— 'About Delius', in Peter Warlock [Philip Heseltine], *Frederick Delius* (London: Bodley Head, 1923, rev. edition 1952), pp. 170–80.

Grieg, Edvard: *Artikler og taler*, ed. Øystein Gaukstad (Oslo: Gyldendal, 1957).

—— *Samlede Verker* (Frankfurt: C.F. Peters, 1977–95).

—— *Brev til Frants Beyer 1872–1907*, ed. Finn Benestad and Bjarne Kortsen (Oslo: Universitetsforlaget, 1993).

—— *Dagbøker 1865, 1866, 1905, 1906 og 1907*, ed. Finn Benestad (Bergen: Bergen Offentlige Bibliotek, 1993).

—— *Edvard Griegs Briefwechsel*, ed. Klaus Henning Oelmann (Egelsbach: Hänsel-Hohenhausen, 1994).

—— *Edvard Grieg: Briefwechsel mit dem Musikverlag C.F. Peters (1863–1907)*, ed. Finn Benestad and Hella Brock (Frankfurt: Peters, 1997).

—— *Edvard Grieg und Julius Röntgen. Briefwechsel 1883–1907*, ed. Finn Benestad and Hanna de Vries Stavland (Amsterdam: Koninklijke Vereniging voor Nederlandse Muziekgeschiedenis, 1997).

—— *Brev i utvalg 1862–1907*, ed. Finn Benestad, 2 vols. (Oslo: Aschehoug, 1998).

—— *Letters to Colleagues and Friends*, ed. and trans. Finn Benestad and William H. Halverson (Columbus: Peer Gynt Press, 2000).

—— *Diaries, Articles, Speeches*, ed. and trans. Finn Benestad and William H. Halverson (Columbus: Peer Gynt Press, 2001).

Grimley, Daniel M.: 'Berwald, Franz', in *The New Grove Dictionary of Music and Musicians*, ed. Stanley Sadie (London: Macmillan, 2001).

—— *Grieg: Music, Landscape and Norwegian Identity* (Woodbridge: Boydell and Brewer, 2006).

—— *Carl Nielsen and the Idea of Modernism* (Woodbridge: Boydell, 2010).

—— '"In the Mood": *Peer Gynt* and the Affective Landscapes of Grieg's *Stemninger*, op. 73', *19th-Century Music*, 40 (2016).

Harrison, Daniel: *Harmonic Function in Chromatic Music: A Renewed Dualist Theory and an Account of Its Precedents* (Chicago: University of Chicago Press, 1994).

Hauptmann, Moritz: *The Nature of Harmony and Metre* (London: Swan Sonnenschein, 1888).

Hold, Trevor: 'Grieg, Delius, Grainger and a Norwegian Cuckoo', *Tempo*, 203 (1998), 11–20.

Helmholtz, Hermann von: *On the Sensations of Tone as a Physiological Basis for the Theory of Music*, trans. Alexander J. Ellis (New York: Dover, 1954).

Hepokoski, James: *Sibelius: Symphony No. 5* (Cambridge: Cambridge University Press, 1993).

Horton, John: 'Musical Personality and Style', in Gerald Abraham (ed.), *Edvard Grieg: A Symposium* (London: Lindsay Drummond, 1948), pp. 111–27.

—— *Grieg (The Master Musicians)* (London: Dent, 1974).

Hyer, Brian: 'Tonality', in Thomas Christensen (ed.), *The Cambridge History of Western Music Theory* (Cambridge: Cambridge University Press, 2002), pp. 726–52.

Jarrett, Sandra: *Edvard Grieg and His Songs* (Aldershot: Ashgate, 2003).

Jersild, Jørgen: *De funktionelle principper i romantikkens harmonik: belyst med udgangspunkt i César Franck's harmoniske stil* (Copenhagen: Wilhelm Hansen, 1970).

Johansen, David Monrad: *Edvard Grieg*, trans. Madge Robertson (Princeton: Princeton University Press, 1938).

Kinderman, William and Krebs, Harald (eds.): *The Second Practice of Nineteenth-Century Tonality* (Lincoln, NE: University of Nebraska Press, 1996).

Kleiberg, Ståle: 'Grieg's "Slåtter", Op. 72: Change of Musical Style or New Concept of Nationality?', *Journal of the Royal Musical Association*, 121 (1996), 46–57.

Kreft, Ekkehard: *Griegs Harmonik* (Frankfurt: Peter Lang, 2000).

Kurth, Ernst: *Die Voraussetzungen der theoretischen Harmonik und der tonalen Darstellungssysteme* (Habilitationsschrift: University of Bern, 1913).

—— *Romantische Harmonik und ihre Krise in Wagners 'Tristan'* (Bern: Paul Haupt, 1920).

—— *Selected Writings*, ed. and trans. Lee A. Rothfarb (Cambridge: Cambridge University Press, 1991).

Lerdahl, Fred and Jackendoff, Ray: *A Generative Theory of Tonal Music* (Cambridge: MIT Press, 1983).

Lewin, David: 'Cohn Functions', *Journal of Music Theory*, 40 (1996), 181–216.

Lewis, Christopher O.: *Tonal Coherence in Mahler's Ninth Symphony* (Ann Arbor: UMI Research Press, 1984).

McCreless, Patrick: 'Elgar and Theories of Chromaticism', in Julian Rushton and J.P.E. Harper-Scott (eds.), *Elgar Studies* (Cambridge: Cambridge University Press, 2007), pp. 1–49.

Massengale, James: '*Haugtussa*: from Garborg to Grieg', *Scandinavian Studies*, 53 (1981), 131–53.

Pople, Anthony: 'Using Complex Set Theory for Tonal Analysis: An Introduction to the *Tonalities* Project', *Music Analysis*, 23 (2004), 153–94.

Proctor, Gregory: 'Technical Bases of Nineteenth-Century Chromatic Tonality' (PhD diss., Princeton University, 1978).

Rameau, Jean-Philippe: *Génération harmonique, ou Traité de musique théorique et pratique* (Paris: Prault fils, 1737).

Rehding, Alexander: *Hugo Riemann and the Birth of Modern Musical Thought* (Cambridge: Cambridge University Press, 2003).

Réti, Rudolph: *Tonality, Atonality, Pantonality: A Study of Some Trends in Twentieth Century Music* (London: Barries and Rockliff, 1958).

Riemann, Hugo: *Musikalische Syntaxis* (Leipzig: Breitkopf & Härtel, 1877).

—— 'Grieg', *Musik-Lexikon*, fourth edition (Leipzig: Max Hesse Verlag, 1894), pp. 399–400.

Röntgen, Julius: *Grieg* (The Hague: J. Philip Kruseman, 1930).

Samson, Jim: *Music in Transition: A Study of Tonal Expansion and Atonality, 1900–1920* (London: Dent, 1977).

Sawyer, Frank J.: 'The Tendencies of Modern Harmony as Exemplified in the Works of Dvořák and Grieg', *Proceedings of the Musical Association*, 22 (1895–6), 53–88.

Schenker, Heinrich: *Harmony*, ed. Oswald Jones, trans. Elizabeth Mann Borgese (Chicago: University of Chicago Press, 1954).

Schjelderup-Ebbe, Dag: *A Study of Grieg's Harmony, with Special Reference to His Contributions to Musical Impressionism* (Oslo: J.G. Tanum, 1953).

—— 'Neue Ansichten über die früheste Periode Edvard Griegs', *Dansk Aarbog for Musikforskning*, 1 (1961), 61–8.

—— *Edvard Grieg, 1858–1867: With Special Reference to the Evolution of His Harmonic Style* (Oslo/London: Universitetsforlaget/Allen & Unwin, 1964).

—— CD liner notes to Edvard Grieg, Complete Piano Music (Geir Henning Braaten), 12 vols., Victoria VCD19025–35 (1992–3).

—— '"Rett fra kua" – Edvard Griegs *19 norske folkeviser*, op. 66', *Studia Musicologica Norvegica*, 25 (1999), 9–11.

Schoenberg, Arnold: *Fundamentals of Musical Composition*, ed. Gerald Strang and Leonard Stein (London: Faber and Faber, 1967).

—— *Theory of Harmony*, trans. Roy E. Carter (Berkeley: University of California Press, 1978).

Steen-Nøkleberg, Einar: *Grieg på podiet: Til spillende fra en spillende* (Oslo: Solum Forlag, 1992), trans. William H. Halverson as *Onstage with Grieg: Interpreting His Piano Music* (Bloomington and Indianapolis: Indiana University Press, 2007).

Sutcliffe, W. Dean: 'Grieg's Fifth: The Linguistic Battleground of "Klokkeklang"', *Musical Quarterly*, 80 (1996), 161–81.

Swinden, Kevin J.: 'Toward Analytic Reconciliation of Outer Form, Harmonic Prolongation and Function', *College Music Symposium*, 45 (2005), 108–23.

Taruskin, Richard: 'Nationalism', in *The New Grove Dictionary of Music and Musicians*, ed. Stanley Sadie (London: Macmillan, 2001).

Taylor, Benedict: 'Modal Four-note Pitch Collections in the Music of Dvořák's American Period', *Music Theory Spectrum*, 32 (2010), 44–59.

—— 'Temporality in Russian Music and the Notion of Development', *Music & Letters*, 94 (2013), 78–118.

—— 'Monotonality and Scalar Modulation in Sibelius's *Tapiola*', unpublished paper, presented at the 'Music and the Nordic Breakthrough' conference, University of Oxford, 1 September 2015.

Tymoczko, Dmitri: 'Scale Networks and Debussy', *Journal of Music Theory*, 48 (2004), 219–94.

—— *A Geometry of Music: Harmony and Counterpoint in the Extended Common Practice* (New York: Oxford University Press, 2011).

—— 'The Generalized Tonnetz', *Journal of Music Theory*, 56 (2012), 1–52.

Yang, Jing-Mao: *Das 'Grieg Motiv' – Zur Erkenntnis von Personalstil und musikalischem Denken Edvard Griegs* (Kassel: G. Bosse, 1998).

Digital Archives

Edvard Grieg Samlingen, Bergen Offentlige Bibliotek, accessible online at http://bergenbibliotek.no/digitale-samlinger/grieg/.

Index of Grieg's works cited

Posthumously Published Works without Opus Number

General Index